PROFESSIONAL ISSUES IN EDUCATION

NUMBER FIFTEEN

EARLY EDUCATION
THE QUALITY DEBATE

PROFESSIONAL ISSUES IN EDUCATION

PROFESSIONAL ISSUES IN EDUCATION

GORDON KIRK *editors* ROBERT GLAISTER

EARLY EDUCATION: THE QUALITY DEBATE

edited by
JOYCE WATT

with contributions from
Joyce Watt
Margaret M. Clark
Marion Flett and Gill Scott
Wendy Dignan, Moira Morrison and Joyce Watt
Esther Read
Annette Holman and Sue Kleinberg
J. Eric Wilkinson and Christine Stephen

SCOTTISH ACADEMIC PRESS
EDINBURGH

Published by
Scottish Academic Press
56 Hanover Street, Edinburgh EH2 2DX

© 1994 Scottish Academic Press Ltd

First published 1994
ISBN 0 7073 0739 2

British Library Cataloguing in Publication data

A catalogue record of this book is available from the British Library.

Typeset by Trinity Typesetting, Edinburgh.

CONTENTS

EDITORIAL INTRODUCTION

The title of this series intends to signal its three main features. Firstly, its general area is education. That term, however, means more than schooling, more than a narrowly instrumental view of a process, and extends beyond the limited notion of an institutional base for activities. Secondly, the topics chosen are matters which excite a good deal of interest and concern, mainly, but not exclusively, because they involve change and development. They are matters on which widely differing views are held: in that sense they are issues. Finally, the series will explore ideas and principles which relate directly to educational practice and to the context in which practices are developed and debated. In that sense the issues raised are professional.

The last few years have seen very significant developments in Scottish education. Much change has taken place so quickly that the process of development has been masked. Equally, practitioners are so busy with the implementation of change in their own practice that they are unaware of developments around the country. If the full benefit from change is to be realised, it is necessary to feed both review and analysis of the process and the product back into the system. This series is an attempt to realise that objective.

The topics will be issues which arise in Scotland, are of critical concern in Scotland, but which will be documented and discussed in a way which makes them equally accessible to an audience furth of Scotland. Indeed, each volume is intended to contribute to the wider educational debate and to inform and enliven the critical discussion of changes in educational practice in Britain and elsewhere. The series should not be seen as a collection of research reports, but rather each volume should draw on research findings and other appropriate resources to offer a readable lively and rigorous analysis of the issues involved.

This series has already featured two volumes in early education. In 1990, Joyce Watt's *Early Education: The Current Debate* provided a wide-ranging analysis of issues in the field. In 1992, in a companion volume, Helen Penn undertook the critical evaluation of the Strathclyde under-fives initiative. Since these volumes appeared, early education has become an area of even more vigorous debate and its proponents continue to urge the critical importance of stronger investment in the education of our youngest children. At the same time, educational discussion has come to be dominated by such issues as accountability, quality, and value for money. It is appropriate, then, that in this volume Dr Watt, herself a leading authority, should assemble a distinguished group of specialists to analyse quality and its enhancement in the context of early education.

PROFESSOR GORDON KIRK
(Moray House Institute of Education)

DR ROBERT GLAISTER
(The Open University)

PREFACE

'Early education' has long had a legitimate pride in the quality of the educational experiences it offers to young children. Given the inequalities in provision, however, particularly at the under-fives level, the public debate has too often focused disproportionately on resources and the availability of places to the relative neglect of the debate on quality.

While questions of resources and availability have certainly not been resolved, the 'quality debate' is now high on the educational agenda. The reasons are not hard to find. First, issues of quality now dominate the educational debate in Britain at every level and early education has to be, and be seen to be, part of that wider discussion. Second, profound political, educational and social changes in society generally, which are having a major impact on how we view the education of young children, are forcing us – rightly – to ask: how are these changes affecting the quality of the educational and social experiences we offer to children and how can we work constructively for the best possible educational deal for children and their families?

The authors in the present volume tackle different aspects of that question as they view it from their own professional perspective:

> how does the 'quality debate' apply to early education?
> what contribution has been made by research to the quality of the educational experiences offered to young children?
> what is, or might be the impact of the Scottish 5–14 curriculum guidelines?

how can we provide quality for both children and
their parents?

what does collaboration between the public and
the voluntary sectors mean and how might it
lead to better quality services?

what is likely to be the impact of new training
initiatives on the quality of services? and,

how do we assess quality in early education?

All contributors write with the authority of many years
experience in the field of early education in Scotland and,
in many cases, also with an international perspective. One
thing is certainly clear: the issues they raise go well beyond
the Scottish and even the British context.

I am very grateful to all who have contributed to this
volume, not just for the quality of their work but also for
the willingness they showed to be involved. As editor, I am
also very appreciative of their efficiency and cooperation
throughout, particularly in responding to my, sometimes
unreasonable, deadlines. It has been a great pleasure to
work with them all.

I would also like to thank Mrs Margaret Sinclair,
secretary in the Department of Education, University of
Aberdeen, for her skill, efficiency and patience in helping
me to put this volume together.

Joyce Watt, July 1994

LIST OF AUTHORS

Margaret M Clark is Emeritus Professor of Education of the University of Birmingham.

Wendy Dignan is an Adviser in Nursery/Primary Education in Lothian Region.

Marion Flett is a Lecturer in the Department of Social Sciences in Glasgow Caledonian University.

Annette Holman is Regional Adviser, Pre-Five Services, for Strathclyde Regional Council.

Sue Kleinberg is School Experience Coordinator for the BEd (Honours) degree in Primary Education in the Faculty of Education, University of Strathclyde.

Moira Morrison is a Senior Lecturer in the Department of Primary Education, Northern College.

Esther Read is a free-lance journalist who was, until very recently, editor of the SPPA magazine *Parent to Parent.*

Gill Scott is a Senior Lecturer in the Department of Social Sciences, Glasgow Caledonian University.

Christine Stephen was a Research Fellow in Education at the University of Glasgow.

Joyce Watt is a Reader in Education at the University of Aberdeen.

J. Eric Wilkinson is a Senior Lecturer in Education at the University of Glasgow.

CHAPTER 1

THE QUALITY DEBATE

Joyce Watt

Introduction

It is less than four years since a previous volume in this series, *Early Education: the current debate* (Watt, 1990), was published. The 'current debate' has, however, moved on and, while most of the issues raised in that volume are still pertinent, the context, even in the brief time which has elapsed, is somewhat different.

Certainly many of the same trends are there: most local authorities still struggle to coordinate their 'education' and 'social work' provision and, increasingly, are having to learn not simply to be service providers but also enablers and supporters of the voluntary and private sectors; women with young children increasingly look for their own opportunities in employment, education and leisure activities and are making more demands on child care services; and the diversification of early childhood services as well as the disparities between them have continued.

It is, however, the context of early education which is changing most rapidly. At a broad structural level, the impending reorganisation of local government in Scotland is likely to bring massive organisational and policy changes: the implications of some of these changes are already being felt. There have also been developments at the policy level whose detail and implications could only be surmised four years ago. For example, the National

Curriculum Guidelines, 5-14 (SOED, 1993) have been published, the Children Act (1989) with its mandatory reviews of under-eights services has been implemented, and new training initiatives, particularly Scottish Vocational Qualifications are now proliferating across the country. In addition, the Scottish Office has produced its first report on the under-fives sector for more than 20 years (SOED, 1994) and the largest regions have invested heavily in producing their own working documents on the early years curriculum (Lothian Regional Council, 1992; Strathclyde Regional Council, 1994).

There is another marked difference in the context of the early education debate in 1994. For the first time in many years the debate, particularly as it relates to the expansion of nursery education, has a high political profile. On 19 November 1993, for example, the Newham Parents' Group presented a petition to Westminster arguing on behalf of 106,676 signatories (of whom 16,000 came from Scotland) for the large-scale expansion of nursery education. Again, at the end of the year, the National Commission on Education (NCE, 1993) argued the case for a 'national strategy' for improving early childhood education and care and, in particular, a state requirement on local authorities to ensure that sufficient high quality, publicly-funded nursery education places should be available for all three- and four-year-olds whose parents want it. Questions on the NCE report were raised in the House of Commons (*Hansard*, 14 December, 1993) but the specific recommendations of the report were dismissed.

At the time of writing, (March, 1994) the report sponsored by the Royal Society for the Arts, *Start Right: the importance of early learning* (Ball, 1994), has just been published. Among its many radical proposals are that

...the Government should immediately prepare legislation to create by 1999 a statutory responsibility for the provision of free, high quality, half-day pre-school education for all children from the age of three in an integrated context of extended day care. (Recommendation 12, para. 7.21)

Even more radically, it proposes that for England and Wales

...the Department for Education should give consideration to raising the age at which children begin compulsory full-time schooling from five to six, and transferring the resources released thereby to enable pre-school education ......to be made available for all children aged three to five inclusive. (Recommendation 13, para. 7.21)

To date there has been no opportunity for questions on these radical proposals to be raised in Parliament, but the latter proposal, at least, has been dismissed as 'absurd' by the Secretary of State for Education, John Patten (*Today* Programme, Radio 4, 17 March 1994).

The more general debate, however, is lively and will continue. There is every sign that the provision of early education will remain on the political agenda at least until the next general election and that it will figure in the manifestos of all major parties. Pressed to reveal the scale of interest and the number of recent representations to the Minister from MPs on the issue of nursery education, a government spokesman recently confirmed:

My Right Honourable Friend has received a large number of representations on nursery education in recent months. (*Hansard*, 1 February, 1994)

That trend is likely to continue and grow.

But expansion of provision of all kinds must take account of quality of provision. 'Quality' is now given a more overt and explicit place in the debate than it had in 1990.

The reasons for that are not hard to find and they are inter-related. First, there are genuine worries that, as demands are made for vastly increased levels of provision without ad-equate resources being made available, a concern for provi-sion for its own sake will overtake concerns for the quality of what is being provided, and almost any provision will be seen as better than no provision at all. At the same time, there is also the danger that, in encouraging ever greater diversifica-tion of provision we may lose sight of the 'quality criteria' which all early education services ought to meet (House of Commons Committee, 1988, para. 5.3). The Rumbold Com-mittee, set up explicitly to examine issues of quality in the educational experiences being offered to children aged 3 to 4, stated its concerns quite explicitly:

> ...... we believe that there is a need, made the more urgent by the rapid pace of current change and devel-opment within the education system as a whole, to raise the quality of a good deal of existing provision. (DES, 1990, para.8)

The second reason why issues of quality are now given a more overt place in the early education debate is that the discussion of quality in all public services is now an integral part of the social and political climate in which we live. All political parties subscribe to 'high quality' public services, although their perceptions of what constitutes quality, how it is to be achieved, and of how the 'quality debate' is to be generated and by whom, differ markedly according to their different value positions.

Quality in public services, including early education, has then a high profile in the present political climate reflecting not only a belief in quality for its own sake but a belief on the part of the present government that consumers should be aware of their rights to demand high quality services and should have the power through mar-ket forces to ensure that high quality services will survive while others will perish. The Citizens' Charter and The Parents' Charter exemplify the government's position on the role of the consumer in other contexts: how it relates to the development of quality services in early education is, however, another matter. We return to this later. For the moment we note simply that the context of the early education debate has changed, that it has a higher political profile than it has had for many years, and that there is a new emphasis on quality. What then does this mean for early education services themselves?

Quality services

As in the previous volume in this series (Watt, 1990) we make no distinction between the 'care' and 'education' of young children, assuming that each is part of the other; without good quality care good learning cannot happen, and a group which is not intent in encouraging children's learning to the full cannot be said to be providing good quality care. The term 'early education' is therefore taken to encompass all groups which provide such a service for children from birth to around the age of 8: nursery schools and classes, primary schools, playgroups, day care centres, family centres, community nurseries and private nurseries including child-minding establishments. Our starting point is, therefore, that 'early education' encompasses a very wide range of services, that each form of the service will differ in its aims, priorities and practice, but that they will all have in common a commitment, albeit in different ways, to providing the best possible care and education for the young children for whom they are responsible.

It is a truism that different perceptions of what constitutes quality are based on different value systems:

Any approach to assessing quality must be preceded by a working through of what we believe matters, what we are trying to achieve and how we will reconcile competing or conflicting goals (Elfer and Wedge, 1992 p 53).

This is true at every level of the early education system. At the level of government, both national and local, the debate about quality in early education cannot be separated from the debate about the level of priority this sector of education should be given and the extent to which it is seen to 'matter'. Value systems are reflected in government commitment or lack of commitment to early education in comparison with other priorities as they see them. Reports from both the House of Commons Committee (1988) and the Royal Society of Arts (Ball,1994) in their arguments for greater support to be given to early education make this point forcibly:

> We recognise that in a world of scarce resources it is not enough to say something is very valuable, and we have considered it equally important to demonstrate why it is particularly vital now (House of Commons, 1988, para. 9.2)

> ...... it is important to establish that the debate is more about priorities than resources. Developed nations do not discuss what they value highest ...... clean water, immunisation, disability benefits, national security or the costs of elections and parliament. The importance of early learning is such that it belongs on this list (Ball, 1994, para. 4.18).

The 'quality debate', then, starts with politicians at both national and local levels determining the place which early education should hold within their scale of priorities and the expectations they have of it and then resourcing it accordingly.

The next stage, however, has to be to define 'quality'. Why is it important to do this? Elfer and Wedge (1992) suggest that one of the main purposes of trying to define quality in early education is that through this kind of process we can be clear what each different kind of service is offering. Within a broad policy consensus of what constitutes quality in early education, different services - nursery schools, playgroups, family centres *etc* - need to determine the values on which their own service is based and on that build their own approach to quality. At the level of the individual institution - the particular play-group, nursery class or day care centre - the same kind of process should operate, reflecting the overall priorities and values of the service as a whole but incorporating those which reflect their own individual characteristics. This then allows assessments of their quality to be made, not by comparing one kind of service with another, but by comparing performance against the criteria which indi-vidual services and groups have set for themselves.

Another important reason for defining quality, high-lighted by Elfer and Wedge (1992), is the contemporary emphasis on ensuring the economic value of services, the 'value for money' argument. Certainly the need to justify expenditure on public services should always be taken for granted and early education should have no qualms on these grounds. The RSA report (Ball, 1994) is unequivocal on its own evidence that

> ...... investment in high quality early education pro-vides a worthwhile economic return to society. (para. 2.21, h)

Both these arguments for the importance of defining quality in early education assume, but do not make ex-plicit, what must be the most important argument of all - that we have a moral obligation as a society to ensure the best possible conditions for children's learning in all its forms. The SOED report (1994) reminds us forcefully that for young children it is not likely to be an option between good learning and no learning at all, but an option between good learning and learning which may have seriously negative consequences:

> Staff need to recognise that babies and children will always be learning and that they must therefore guard against poor quality or negative experiences from which only poor quality or negative learning can follow. (para. 4.27)

This still, of course, leaves us with the most difficult question of all - what is quality? Theories on the nature of quality, quality assurance and quality management from the world of industry (Juran, 1974: Crosby, 1979; Deming, 1986; Garvin, 1988) and a recent useful attempt to relate these theories to the welfare services (Pfeffer and Coote, 1991) leave us in no doubt that there are many different approaches to defining quality according to the purpose and the context served. Pfeffer and Coote outline four approaches : the 'traditional' approach which aims to convey prestige in the quality product and claim advantage over competitors; the 'scientific/expert' approach which aims to meet standards set by experts; the 'managerial/ excellence' approach which aims to measure customer satisfaction; and the 'consumerist' approach which aims to make the customer more powerful. They argue that all these approaches, apart from the first, have a place in welfare services and they can co-exist, but they need to be adapted since, as they have operated and been understood, they do not sufficiently distinguish between the very different worlds of commerce and welfare.

> Once 'quality' leaves the commercial world, rules and relationships change and it loses its clarity of purpose. Since it is no longer clear what it is for, it can take on a host of different meanings and be used for a range of purposes depending on who is deploying it - and why. (p. 31)

That said, it is important for early education to recognise some of the main criteria against which quality is to be judged. Again the RSA report (Ball, 1994) gives a lead. According to its findings and deliberations, quality in early education overall is a reflection of the individual quality of the curriculum offered, the selection, training and continuity of the staff, the staff:child ratios, and (of lesser importance) the quality of the accommodation and equipment and the role played by parents. (para. 2.10) Common features of good practice are listed as:

> clear aims and objectives;
> a broad, balanced and developmentally appropriate curriculum;
> a variety of learning experiences which are active, relevant and enjoyable;
> warm and positive relationships;
> a well planned, stimulating, secure and healthy environment; and
> a commitment to equal opportunities and social justice for all.

Still important but of lower priority are:

> systematic planning, assessment and record keeping;
> satisfactory adult:child ratios, continuity of care and consistent staff development;
> partnership with parents and family and liaison with the community; and
> effective procedures for monitoring and evaluating the quality of practice. (paras. 6.4 - 6.11)

This is a list with which few in early education are likely to disagree fundamentally although they might add other criteria or dispute order and priorities. Flett and Scott (this volume), for example, would add that quality is

reflected in the way early education plans for the complementary needs of mothers and children:

> Good quality provision will seek to meet the needs of
> both children and mothers ...... It will never suggest that
> these needs are in opposition to one another. (p. 61)

It is important that such lists are available, however, to
inform the debate. What also matters is that those who
work in the field of early education, in whatever capacity,
should be aware of the value systems and the evidence on
which such lists and any claim to 'quality' are based, so that
they can recognise the purposes which lie behind defining
quality in particular ways.

Other important questions remain: how are the criteria
for quality to be drawn up at each level and by whom? how
is quality to be assessed and by whom? how is quality to be
developed? Some of these questions are explored in detail
by Wilkinson and Stephen later in this volume and are
therefore not pursued further here. We conclude this
section, therefore, by discussing briefly some of the new
opportunities for promoting quality in early education as
well as some of the barriers which still seem to exist.

Some of the new opportunities are obvious. One of the
most significant developments in promoting quality in
early education, for example, must be the Children Act
(1989) which has made it mandatory on local authorities
not only to draw up their own criteria for quality services
and to review those services regularly, but to bring together a wide range of workers from the public, voluntary
and private sectors in implementing the process. Training
needs will also be identified and new training opportunities should be forthcoming (see Holman and Kleinberg,
this volume). Also, while there have been many false starts
and much misunderstanding (see Read, this volume) the
public and voluntary sectors are working more closely
together and learning to support each other in more

positive ways. That must be in the interests of quality for the service as a whole.

Despite these positive trends, it is also clear that there are still many barriers to quality in early education. There can be little doubt that in the drive for expansion without adequate resources and the proliferation of many kinds of *ad hoc* groups, quality is being sorely compromised. Other problems are identified in the present volume: for example, Holman and Kleinberg outline some of the problems for quality associated with the training of early years workers; Dignan, Morrison and Watt express concern at the lack of support given to early years teachers; and Flett and Scott argue strongly that we have still a very long way to go in providing a quality service which provides for the complementary needs of children and their mothers.

At the level of practice, the recent SOED report (1994), while providing an overall picture of positive practice, also identifies significant problems. Some relate to lack of staff skill and understanding, others to lack of resources, and others to what Inspectors see as an inability on the part of staff, for whatever reason, to get priorities right:

> ...... there were significant differences in the skills staff brought both to their evaluation of the quality of the children's talk and to their knowledge of the roles adults could play to enhance quality. (para. 6.55)
>
> ...... lack of space or resources or lack of knowledge on the part of staff led to children spending excessive amounts of time at play with jigsaws, posting boxes matching games and table-top activities. (para. 6.76)

Difficulties in making effective provision for children's language development were noted when:

> the staff concentrated more on the physical care of their charges and gave talk and communication a low priority;

staff worked with so many children in the course of a day that the focus of their attention was on the provision of activities to keep the children occupied and they did not spend sufficient time with individuals......

the programme did not give the children a sufficient number of interesting experiences for them to talk about ...... (para. 6.54)

Lack of skill and understanding on the part of staff and lack of resources are clear barriers to quality. Just as important, however, are barriers which arise from ill-conceived assumptions on the part of staff and ill-informed attitudes towards families and the role of parents in the education of their children. Clark (this volume), for example, reminds us how research in early education has faced us with the uncomfortable truth that some children enjoy more enriching language experiences with their parents at home than they do in some nursery schools. Tharp and Gallimore (1991) in their discussion of 'assisted learning' also challenge some professional assumptions:

Schools have much to learn by examining the informal pedagogy of everyday life. The principles of good teaching are not different for school than for home and community. When true teaching is found in schools it observes the same principles that good teaching exhibits in informal settings. (p. 42)

And tellingly:

Most parents do not need to be trained to assist performance; most teachers do. (p. 58)

None of this is to question the importance of professional teachers. Dignan, Morrison and Watt (this volume) argue a strong case for recognising the importance and complexity of the teacher's task; and The House of Commons Report (1988) claimed:

(During the visit of the committee to the United States) we noted that, where the quality of education was of a high standard, one or more appropriately qualified teachers were on the staff...... The same is true in England. (para. 5.14)

Nor does it question the quality of what is offered in most professionally-run groups such as nursery schools and classes. Ball (1994), for example, presents ample evidence of the effectiveness of 'high quality' groups which are professionally run. What it does question, however, is the assumption that any one designated group of people have a monopoly of quality in their interactions with children and that a professionally-run group will inevitably offer a higher quality service (see also Wilkinson and Stephen, this volume).

Professionals also need to take seriously Read's challenge (this volume) that those who are critical of the voluntary sector's lack of training and experience to develop the under-fives curriculum should look at their own skills in working with parents and ask themselves whether their training and experience equip them to pursue this aspect of their work effectively. Work with parents is complex although it is rewarding, but its quality is in serious doubt where staff, from whatever sector, make ill-conceived assumptions about parents and their role, or think at only a superficial level about what is meant by the somewhat hackneyed phrase 'parent involvement'. Ball (1994) should make us all think again when, in emphasising the critical role to be played by parents in early education, he says:

...... neither of the terms 'involvement' or even 'partnership' quite hits the mark. It is as if we were to talk of the mother's involvement or *partnership* with the midwife at the birth of the child. (para. 5.2)

Our final 'barrier' to quality is, however, more pervasive. It is a central part of this argument that we will never develop quality in early education in this country until those services are contextualised within a national policy framework which can be implemented with discretion at local authority level and reflected in individual ways in the policies and practices of each service. The call for a national policy, particularly in under-fives services, is far from new and has been articulated most recently by Cohen and Fraser (1991) and by Pugh (1992). Cohen and Fraser argue in their review of 'childcare' ('a generic term encompassing care, education and play' p.58), that

> it is up to government to take the lead responsibility by setting out and implementing a national child care policy. (p 9)

and Pugh makes the strong plea:

> ...... in the interests of providing children with continuity and coherence and in making the most efficient use of scarce resources, ... a coordinated policy, with mechanisms for joint planning, management and review, must surely be a first priority. (p. 11)

To date there is, however, no such clearly articulated policy and it is important to ask why this should be and what the implications are for the quality of early education in this country.

Policy and quality

At the most general level it is perhaps arguable that there are national policy guidelines on early education. At the under-fives level, at least, there is a consensus on the importance of early learning through play, on working through parents and families, and there is a general commitment to the expansion of services (House of Com-

mons, 1988; DES 1990; SOED, 1994). Whether there is
that same commitment to the play curriculum in the early
years of the primary school is another matter.

There is, however, no commitment to a national policy
on the organisation and coordination of under-fives services, an issue on which government has been pressed since
the mid 1970s (Pugh,1988). Despite the fact that Strathclyde Region in Scotland pioneered the total integration
of under-fives services in the mid 1980s (Strathclyde Regional Council, 1985) and to date ten local authorities in
England have now followed suit (Penn,1994), central
government has persistently refused to give a national
lead on the issue. The Rumbold Committee (DES, 1990)
itself recommended it but to no avail:

> We believe that the achievement of better local coor-
> dination would be greatly helped if central government
> gave a clear lead, setting a national framework within
> which local development could take place. (para. 215)

On one specific issue - the expansion of nursery education - it became clear at the end of 1993 that not only was
there no clear policy, there was no Cabinet consensus. In
its response to the proposals of the National Commission
on Education (NCE, 1993) a government spokesman
stated:

> The National Commission's proposals for free state
> nursery education for all 3 and 4-year-olds conflicts with
> our policy of choice and diversity of provision which
> best meets the varied needs of children and their
> parents. It is also unrealistic in resource terms. (*Hansard,*
> 14 December, 1993)

Subsequent to this statement, however, Prime Minister
John Major indicated informally, and no doubt with an
eye to its electoral potential, that he was positively dis-
posed to the expansion of nursery education. This pro-

voked Ann Taylor, Labour spokesperson on Education to demand that the minister should 'clear up the Government's shambles on nursery education' and she asked directly in the House:

> Do Education Ministers back the Prime Minister? Do they favour universal nursery education?

The reply she was given was a quotation from the speech given by John Patten, Secretary of State for Education, to the North of England Education conference at the end of 1993 which claimed consensus but stated the government position in only the most general terms:

> The Prime Minister and I are therefore keen to find ways of helping to extend over time the amount of nursery schooling available (*Hansard*, 1 February, 1994)

For one section of early education, of course, the present government has stated its policy position clearly. As far as children of primary school age are concerned, the far-reaching changes of the last decade in terms of the school curriculum, assessment, parental choice of school, the management of schools and changes to teacher training have affected young children just as much as, perhaps even more than, any other age group.

It is at the under-fives level, especially, that we have the policy vacuum. And yet that is not quite true either. There is a 'policy' that, for the most part, central government will not become involved except inasmuch as it will encourage the expansion of services, and will set up procedures to ensure quality and cost effectiveness. 'Choice' and 'diversity' are key concepts, but it remains with local authorities to establish their own priorities and their own policies.

> The Government's policy is to promote choice, diversity, quality and cost-effectiveness in the provision of preschool education and to extend the amount of such

education available ...... We are exploring ways of add-
ing still further, as resources allow, to the choice already
available to parents from all sources - public, private and
voluntary. (*Hansard,* 14 January, 1994)

This echoes a statement by John Patten, now Secretary of
State for Education, made almost ten years ago:

Day care will continue to be primarily a matter of
private arrangement between parents and private and
voluntary resources except where there are special
needs. (*Hansard,* March 18, 1985)

Behind these statements lies the clear philosophy of the
present Conservative Government that the level of state
services should be controlled and their role changed, that
the voluntary and private sectors are to be encouraged,
and that under-fives services, like so many other public
services, are to be open to the influence of market forces.
Quality will be determined and controlled by the consumers who will choose what they want in an open market. By
giving consumers 'rights' including the right to compensation and redress, consumers as individuals will attain
power over what state services offer and this will lead to
enhanced quality for everyone.

This position is in marked contrast to that in most of the
rest of Europe where the level of pre-school services is very
much higher, and they attract more public investment
within national policies committed to the public support
of young children and their families (Moss, 1994).

The United Kingdom is unique in depending so
heavily in its provision for children over 3 on playgroups, early admission to primary school and a 'shift
system' for nursery education. (p. 113)

Pointing out the irony that the United Kingdom has the
highest growth rate of female employment and the lowest

rate of day care, Pugh (1992) also makes the point:

> In contrast to the rest of Europe, day care in the United Kingdom is seen as a private matter to be resolved by parents who are either expected to make their own arrangements with a relative or buy in services in the market place. (p. 14)

There are, however, several practical reasons why a 'policy' for early education based on the market place is, in effect, no policy at all. First, the market place philosophy depends on being able to identify the consumer. It is easy to define the consumer in the supermarket, it is much less easy in the welfare services such as early education. As Martin (1986) points out:

> If the identity of the consumer cannot be defined by who pays for the service, it may be difficult to decide who the consumer is. (p. 189)

In the case of early education, defining the consumer is quite difficult: is it the child? or the family? Or, if we accept on the evidence of long-term studies that the effectiveness of high quality early education shows itself most clearly in children's increased self esteem, self reliance and confidence (Sylva, 1994), is it not at least arguable that the 'client' of early education is the community, or even society as a whole? That is not to reduce the importance of the child and family as consumer or client but to place the notion of consumerism in a broader setting. As Pfeffer and Coote (1993) point out, the context of consumerism in the welfare services is very different from that in the world of business and commerce, not least because, as we have seen, there is often more than one customer involved. Indeed, services may be placed in the public sector in the first place just because there is more than one customer involved.

Second, while most people in early education would support the principle of choice, the notion that families in

the United Kingdom do have choice in the early education services they use is quite wrong. While there are some
areas where a variety of alternative forms of provision exist
side by side, in many areas families count themselves
fortunate if they can find a place at all, particularly in
nursery education. The chances of finding a place still
depend on where you live, whether you can provide
transport, whether and how much you can afford to pay,
whether you can accommodate the hours offered, or
whether you can argue 'special need'. The chances are
slim for most parents of being able to choose among
alternatives and find a place for their child in the kind of
provision they want, with a curriculum they like, with the
hours they want, at the age they want their child to start,
and with the kind of relationships with parents which they
find supportive. Most take what, if anything, is available.
Certainly the system may offer diversity, but valid choice is
another matter.

   Third, the consumer model assumes the possibility of
redress or compensation if 'quality' is poor. 'Redress' or
'compensation' for the consumers of early education is
much more difficult, however, than it would be in the
world of commerce where shoddy goods can be returned
and compensation made. This is not to say we should not
take very seriously the problem of poor quality services
and listen constructively to what consumers, however
defined, have to say, but how can the individual consumer
– the child or the family – be 'compensated' for poor
learning experiences other than to be satisfied that every
effort is being made to improve the system for the future?
Behind this problem, of course, lies the even greater
problem which we explored briefly in the previous section
- what constitutes a 'high quality' or a 'low quality' service
and how can consumers 'show' that they have experienced a poor service in the same way as they can show if
they have bought defective goods? The problem is exacer-
bated by the fact that consumers of services make judg-

ments based not simply on the objective features of the service they use, but also on the subjective feelings they experience in the process of service delivery. Townsend and Gebhart (1986) distinguish between the 'quality of fact' - the objective standards set for services - and 'quality of perception' as this is seen by the participant in the process. They may or may not be strongly related.

As well as practical objections to the application of the consumerist/market forces philosophy as a way to raise quality in early education, there are also objections of principle. Here we return to the central point in the whole quality debate: that different perceptions of quality are based on different value systems. Those in early education who disagree with the market forces argument on principle do so largely on two grounds.

First, they would argue that all welfare services, and early education in particular, should be based on notions of equality and equal life chances for all children. Pfeffer and Coote (1991) go so far as to say that the purpose of public welfare services is

> ...... to ensure that, as far as possible, everyone has an equal chance to participate in society, to enjoy its fruits, and to realise their own potential. (p. 23)

Services based on market forces, however, are likely to exacerbate inequalities even although policies of 'positive discrimination' on behalf of the disadvantaged may operate in some parts of the system. Pugh (1992) makes the point :

> A policy that leaves service departments to market forces tends to disadvantage the already disadvantaged and (as is now evident in the United States) is vulnerable to changes in the economy. (p. 13)

A policy based on market forces and rampant consumerism cannot easily then accommodate a fundamental concern for equality.

A second reason for rejecting the market forces model in early education is that it puts all its emphasis on the individual consumer, and the power of consumers to raise quality by taking their 'business' elsewhere. But, as Pfeffer and Coote (1991) again argue, while the empowerment of consumers is important, in the field of welfare services we are all not only individual consumers with our own vested interests, we are also citizens in a society which acknowledges our inter-dependence and our communal interest in developing quality services for all. Individual needs are important, but welfare services also have to serve the wider interests of the community as a whole.

The point is well taken in the 'quality debate' in early education. Earlier we raised the question of who constitutes 'the consumer' in early education and we have returned again to the same dilemma. Individuals have a key personal interest in obtaining high quality provision as they see it and this has to be respected and accommodated. But communities have a more general interest in how services meet the needs of the community as a whole, and there is a yet wider interest on the part of society that the investment it makes in its youngest children is not only in their best interests but in the best long-term interests of society itself. Common purposes and individual needs are not incompatible and they have to be reconciled within a policy framework which recognises the legitimacy of both. Competition has no place on this agenda for the promotion of quality services. As Pfeffer and Coote (1991) put it, 'better' should mean 'better than before' and not, as in the market place, 'better than others' (p. 24).

In this discussion of quality in early education, we have so far emphasised two main points. First, there is a legitimate concern for quality in all kinds of early education at the present time and that challenge has to be acknowledged and met. As a society we need to acknowledge not only the strengths of our services but also their weaknesses, and fight for the resources to improve them.

Second, we have argued that quality overall is not possible without a clear policy lead from central government on major issues such as demand, coordination of services, the relationship between the non-statutory under-fives sector and the statutory school sector, and the resource implications of expansion.

Finally, therefore, we come to the obvious but critical point that a quality service can only be built on a policy which itself meets quality criteria. Perceptions of what those quality criteria ought to be will again vary greatly according to different value systems and different scales of priorities but, in a democratic society, certain key features should be taken for granted. Cohen and Fraser (1991), for example, argue that any policy for early education (or 'childcare' the term they use) should be underpinned by the clear acknowledgment that such a policy is in the public interest and that there is a clear relationship between public investment in these services and the potential for economic growth. They then go on to detail the criteria which, as they see it, a national policy of 'quality' has to meet. These include: its acceptance as a key component in a modern welfare system; its ability to encompass 'education' and 'care'; its ability to be responsive, equitable, and serve a range of interests; and its potential to link child care policies with employment provision, and to pay both economic and social benefits (p. 59-60).

Given the importance of the task, the critical question is, of course, who is to contribute to the development of a policy for early education. In a democratic society there can be only one answer to that. Whether we are talking at the level of national government or at the level of the individual playgroup or nursery school, all the 'stakeholders' have a right to their place in the policy-making process. Beyond that, what matters is that those who take on the policy-making mantle think and act not just as individual representatives or consumers but as citizens who are concerned to provide a quality service for all.

The 'quality debate' in early education has a long way to go. This volume, it is hoped, will contribute constructively to that debate, not just in the Scottish context but beyond, since the issues it raises know few national boundaries. It began with a concern that the pace and nature of change in education and in society generally was threatening what many believed was the essence of good early education. Its process of development has revealed many things, not least the need to give 'quality' issues a higher place on the early education agenda. What it has also revealed is that the debate is probably more informed and more lively than it has been for a long time. Increasingly we have a debate not just *about* quality but a debate which itself *exhibits* quality. We hope that the present volume makes a distinctive contribution in both senses to the 'quality debate' in early education in Scotland.

References

Ball, Sir C. (1994) *Start Right: the importance of early learning*. London: Royal Society for the Encouragement of the Arts, Manufacturers and Commerce.

Clark, M. M. (1994) Environments for Young Children's Learning: what can we learn from research? *in* Watt, J. (ed.) *Early Education: the quality debate*. Edinburgh: Scottish Academic Press.

Cohen, B. and Fraser, N. (1991) *Child Care in a Modern Welfare System: towards a New National Policy*. London: Institute for Public Policy Research.

Crosby, P. B. (1979) *Quality is Free*. New York: McGraw-Hill.

Department of Education and Science (1990) *Starting with Quality. The Report of the Committee of Enquiry into the Quality of the Educational Experiences offered to 3- and 4-year-olds* (The Rumbold Report). London: Department of Education and Science.

Deming, W. E. (1986) *Out of the Crisis*. Cambridge, Mass: MIT Press.

Dignan, W. Morrison, M. and Watt, J. (1994) Learning in the early years curriculum, *in* Watt, J. (ed.) *Early Education: the quality debate*. Edinburgh: Scottish Academic Press.

Elfer, P. and Wedge, D. (1992) Defining, measuring and supporting quality, *in* Pugh, C. (ed.) *Contemporary Issues in the Early Years: working collaboratively for children*. London: Paul Chapman and National Children's Bureau

Flett, M. and Scott, G. (1994) Quality for adults: quality for children, *in* Watt, J. (ed.) *Early Education: the quality debate*. Edinburgh: Scottish Academic Press.

Garvin, D. A. (1988) *Managing Quality: the strategic and competitive edge*. New York: Free Press

Holman, A. and Kleinberg, S. (1994) Training for quality in early education, *in* Watt, J. (ed.) *Early Education: the quality debate*. Edinburgh: Scottish Academic Press.

House of Commons Committee (1988) *Educational Provision for the Under Fives*. London: HMSO.

Juran, J. M. (1974) *Quality Control Handbook*, 3rd ed. New York: McGraw-Hill.

Lothian Regional Council (1992) *A Curriculum for the Early Years*. Edinburgh: Lothian Regional Council.

Martin, E. (1986) Consumer evaluation of human services, *Social Policy and Administration*, 20 (3), 195-199.

Moss, P. (1994) Statistics on early childhood services: placing Britain in an international context, *in* Ball, Sir C. *Start Right: the importance of early learning*, Appendix F. London: Royal Society for the Encouragement of the Arts, Manufacturers and Commerce.

National Commission on Education (1993) *Learning to Succeed: a radical look at education today and a strategy for the future*. Report of the Paul Hamlyn Foundation. London: Heinemann.

Penn, H. (1994) Stuck on the nursery slopes, *The Times Educational Supplement (Scotland)* No. 1429, 25 March, p18.

Pfeffer, N. and Coote, A. (1991) *Is Quality Good for You? A critical review of quality assurance in welfare services*. London: Institute for Public Policy Research.

Pugh, G. (1988) *Services for Under Fives: developing a coordinated approach*. London: National Children's Bureau.

Pugh, G. (1992) A policy for early childhood services, *in* Pugh, G. (ed.) *Contemporary Issues in the Early Years: working collaboratively for children*. London: Paul Chapman and National Children's Bureau.

Read, E. (1994) The voluntary and public sectors: a partnership of paranoias? *in* Watt, J. (ed.) *Early Education: the quality debate*. Edinburgh: Scottish Academic Press.

Scottish Office Education Department (1993) *The Structure and Balance of the Curriculum, 5-14*. Edinburgh: HMSO.

Scottish Office Education Department (1994) *Education of Children Under 5 in Scotland*. Edinburgh: SOED.

Strathclyde Regional Council (1985) *Under Fives: Report of the Member/Officer Group*. Glasgow: Strathclyde Regional Council.

Strathclyde Regional Council (1994) *Partners in Learning: 0-5 Curriculum Guidelines. Glasgow: Strathclyde Regional* Council.

Sylva, K. (1994) The impact of early learning on children's later development, *in* Ball, Sir C. *Start Right: the importance of early learning,* Appendix C.

London: Royal Society for the Encouragement of the Arts, Manufacturers and Commerce.

Tharp, R. and Gallimore, R. (1991) A theory of teaching as assisted learning, *in* Light, P. Sheldon, S. and Woodhead, M. (eds.) *Learning to Think.* London: Routledge.

Townsend, P. L. and Gebhart, J. E. (1986) *Commit to Quality.* New York: Wiley.

Watt, J. (1990) *Early Education: the current debate.* Edinburgh: Scottish Academic Press.

CHAPTER 2

ENVIRONMENTS FOR YOUNG CHILDREN'S LEARNING: WHAT CAN WE LEARN FROM RESEARCH?

Margaret M Clark

Introduction

Whatever else it is about, 'quality' in education must be concerned with the 'learning environment' offered to children. How can we improve the quality of the learning environment in early education? Both researchers and practitioners are committed to trying to answer that question.

This chapter looks at the contribution of research, particularly observation research, to the learning environment of young children. It focuses on a few key research studies since the 1970s selected because they have studied children's natural behaviour by 'observing' them through watching or listening to them. It argues that:

(i)   close observation of children's natural behaviour is critical to our understanding of how they learn;

(ii) the findings from observation studies have contributed considerably to our understanding of children's learning and how we can provide better learning opportunities;

(iii) some observation techniques developed in the 're-search domain' can and should be adapted by practitioners so that children's learning environments can be based on the needs of children themselves; and

(iv) researchers and practitioners need to work together if the quality of children's learning environments is to be improved.

The role of research

During their training, no matter how crowded the curriculum, teachers in early education should gain an appreciation of the findings and limitations of relevant research. Furthermore, as professionals, they need a framework within which to assess the value of future research; otherwise they may be either unwilling to accept what are indeed new insights of value to their practice, or they may remain vulnerable to extravagant claims said to come from 'research evidence', where this appears, on the surface, to be impressive. Again, students who see only summaries of research are likely to have an over-simplified, and over-generalised, picture of research findings. They are unlikely to gain an understanding of the decision-making which was required before and throughout each investigation and the consequences of choice of approach, of sample, and of methods of study and analysis.

On the other hand, study of selected researches set in their historical context can be an effective way of showing the relationship of research evidence to policy and practice and perhaps of helping teachers to adopt a research perspective within their own practice (see Clark, 1989).

Responsibility for achieving this, however, lies not only with teachers and teacher educators. If educational researchers are to make impact, they too must recognise their responsibilities. They must learn to:

(i) communicate effectively with lay people, policy-makers and professionals;
(ii) provide information which is sufficiently explicit for

other research workers to repeat a study – all too often it is not possible to know whether two studies contradict each other or can co-exist, because of the lack of relevant detail; and

(iii) regard statistical significance as only one factor in determining the educational value of their findings.

Rarely should a single study be regarded as having educational significance, although successive studies should improve methodology and help to build a body of knowledge. Nor should we look to research to provide ready-made answers to short-term problems. Research workers are best seen as 'expert witnesses', who can influence the climate of opinion. While no more value-free than others, they can perhaps suspend judgment on a number of contemporary issues so that, while not defining what ought to be, they can at least indicate a wider range of potential options and their possible consequences. All the above points are highly relevant to anyone studying the history of research into early education over the past twenty-five years.

This chapter is not the place to provide a comprehensive summary and evaluation of research into early education. A personal commission from The Secretary of State for Education in 1985 required me to 'carry out a critical evaluation of research into the education of under-fives undertaken in recent years' .....

'to assist those who wish to refer to existing research, to guide future policy on research in this area, and ultimately to facilitate better deployment of existing resources'. (Sir Keith Joseph in a written statement in *Hansard* 27.2.85, p. 180)

That report, published as *Children under Five: educational research and evidence,* contains a wealth of research findings in early education from the 1970s through to the mid-80s

(Clark, 1988). Further studies of significance to early education set in their historical context for teachers in training are discussed in the book referred to earlier (Clark, 1989).

The present chapter selects a few studies from that period, most of them well known. It focuses on those studies which were based largely on observation techniques and on a particular age group of children (3-6) within the 'early education' range. It asks the question: what has been learned from these observation studies which might improve the quality of learning environments for children in the transition years between preschool and primary education?

Before we tackle this question, however, it is important to clarify some of the differences between administrative practices in Scotland and England which sometimes obscure understanding of educational issues as children 'start school' north and south of the Border.

The educational setting

Many people in England seem to believe that education in Scotland is traditional, formal and somewhat dated. Others assume that the changes currently being enforced in England and Wales by a succession of Secretaries of State for Education also apply to Scotland. Seldom is reference made either in the national press or on television to the widening gap between the educational systems north and south of the Border. At a time when education in England and Wales has become more rigid and formal, with the curriculum and assessment dictated by central government, the developments in Scotland under the same government are very different. Teachers, advisers and college lecturers have throughout played an important role in planning the curriculum and related assessment in Scotland, unlike their colleagues in England and

Wales who have been allowed little say either in the curriculum, or the national programme of assessment which is coming to dominate the curriculum. What are the key differences in the educational provision in the two systems as these affect the years of 'early education'?

First, in Scotland primary education covers seven rather than six years, with children entering primary school at the beginning of the school year in which they will be five years of age by the end of February. Thus the age range in reception classes is similar throughout Scotland, and at the beginning of the school year is four–and–a–half to five–and–a–half years of age. In contrast, in England and Wales there is wide variation, not only between local authorities, but even between schools. The latest time at which children can enter school is the term after their fifth birthday. However, depending on the number of entry dates to school and the child's date of birth, children may enter reception class when only four years of age. The age range in one reception class may thus be four to five, while in another reception class all the children may be over five years of age. Thus the age range of children in pre-school education, in nursery schools or classes, playgroups or day nurseries in England and Wales will differ greatly depending on these factors. It is important to note that the oldest children in pre-schools in Scotland may be older than any children in such units in England. In contrast, the youngest children in reception classes in England may be six months younger than the youngest in such classes in Scotland.

One reason for stressing these points is that many publications, and even research studies, refer to 'pre-school education' or 'reception classes' without indicating the age group in question. Perhaps the greater danger in Scotland is that we may not stretch our oldest children in the pre-school setting sufficiently; in contrast the danger in England currently may be that not enough account is taken of the relative youth of many children in reception class (even compared to ten or fifteen years ago).

Second, primary school teachers in Scotland train for the age range 3-12 and are required during their training to have practical experience in the pre-school as well as infant and junior departments. This is not true in England. It is to be hoped that even a brief period of practical experience with these different age groups during their training will encourage teachers in primary schools in Scotland to be more sensitive to the needs of all children in their care and to be more knowledgeable of the aims and practices in other stages of early education. Likewise, teachers working in pre-school settings will have had some experience of the curriculum and activities required of children in the later stages of the primary school. Carefully planned observational studies during their practical experience should indeed alert teachers in training to the wide variation in knowledge as well as maturity at each stage, and, equally important, to the overlap between children at different stages of education. Such awareness should enable them to ensure that continuity and challenge are considered in the experiences that are offered to children at each stage of their school career. Some of the findings from observational research studies within which such techniques were developed will be mentioned in the following sections.

Third, in England and Wales, the National Curriculum has been defined in terms of 'core' and 'foundation' subjects, with separate committees appointed to develop the curriculum for each subject, very much in isolation from one another, and with little representation from teachers. This has led to overloading of the curriculum, and, when coupled with national testing at the end of Key Stage 1, when some of the children are not yet seven years of age, is coming to dictate practice in early education.

Recent developments in Scotland, in contrast, are not enshrined in Acts of Parliament with their attendant statutory orders. National tests are only in English and Mathematics with the time of the testing at the teacher's discretion, and National Curriculum Guidelines for the age range 5-14 (see Chapter 4) emphasise the need for breadth and continuity (SOED, 1993). To a Scot like myself, now living south of the Border, it is clear that the teacher in early education in Scotland is empowered to develop a curriculum suited to the needs of the children in his or her charge in ways that are being denied to teachers in the rest of Britain. In Scotland, there should be the opportunity in early education to plan the curriculum, at least in part, around the knowledgeable observation of children. The need to do this is no less critical south of the Border since, in both contexts as we have seen, the age range, as well as the age range of children within any one setting, may vary widely.

Communication in early education

The development of language competence in pre-school children, particularly those from disadvantaged backgrounds, became an important priority and justification for the proposed expansion of pre-school education in the 1970s. Its priority was based on two assumptions both of which must, on the basis of research evidence, now be challenged, or at least seen to be overly simplistic solutions to highly complex problems. First, there was a belief that the lack of language competence shown by some children in a formal test situation, and in school, and their subsequent school failure, could be attributed to a lack of dialogue between them and their parents in the pre-school years. Second, there was the assumption that if such children attended pre-schools with a rich supply of stimulating materials and qualified adults with whom they could interact, they would experience dialogue with these adults that was intellectually demanding, and play experiences which were progressively more challenging (see Clark, 1988, Chapter 2, for a discussion of these issues and further references).

It is very easy for the visitor to a pre-school setting to believe on the basis of general observations that most, if not all, children are enjoying stimulating educational experiences. It is also possible for the visitor to two pre-school establishments whose headteachers express very different philosophies, to believe that the curriculum *as experienced by individual children* in the two settings is very different, which may not be the case. Likewise, it is very tempting to believe that, where a child says little in a school setting, even with sympathetic prompting by well-qualified experienced adults, the child in question is incapable of saying more and will say even less at home. If the parent appears similarly limited in communication, it is tempting to assume that this provides evidence of a causal relationship between the two. Closer study, however, through observation techniques and the judicious use of sensitive radio-microphones, has revealed a rather different picture of the dynamics of interaction in home and in school and how these affect different children.

The importance of observation

Much of the evidence from the research in pre-school units in the 1970s and 1980s was obtained through the use of specially devised observation schedules on which was recorded the length of time spent at various activities by selected target children. Time sampling of target children, and/or observations at specific activities, made it possible to compare and contrast the choice of activities and time spent at these by children of different ages, sex or background. Activities which appear to attract most children, to sustain their interest for long periods of time and lead to more complex play could be identified. The effect of the presence of an adult at an activity could be assessed: whether that appeared to attract more children to the activity (even if the adult were not involved); and whether it led to their spending longer there, to certain children choosing to play near the adult, or others avoiding such activities.

The size of groups in which young children choose to play, and the quality of the play within different sizes of group, could also be studied. The frequency with which adults talk to particular children, the activities at which talk is most frequent, and the extent of 'turn-taking' during a particular episode could be measured. From studies on topics such as these, a great deal of evidence has been accumulated from the programme of research studies in pre-school units in the 1970s and 1980s. This evidence has important implications for practitioners who wish to improve the quality of the environment for learning they offer to young children.

First, a few key points are noted from two important researches using observational techniques in pre-school units, that of Bruner and his colleagues in Oxford (see Sylva, Roy and Painter, 1980), and that based on the work of the Hutts (Hutt, Tyler, Hutt and Christopherson, 1989).

Bruner's colleagues found more complex play arose in activities where there was a clear goal which was appreciated by the children. They also identified the danger that an open-plan free play setting may lead to flitting and distraction and a low level of activity by some children. The Hutts give a picture of children in pre-school units being purposefully engaged, often in activities of their own choice but with frequent interruptions, some children with very limited attention spans, others concentrating on occasion for over an hour. In both so-called 'fantasy play' and play with dry sand a great deal of repetitive and low level play was observed. The most sustained and lively play was found around activities where the child had a 'captive' adult in the vicinity.

Both studies stress the potential for concentration in many young children, and if play is to be complex and sustained, the importance of how activities are organised and the strategic placing of adults. There was little evidence of the hoped-for complex conversation or discussion of past or future events in the pre-school units. The need for planning which encourages more sustained, if less frequent, dialogue between children and adults, and activities which encourage dialogue between peers, has been highlighted by a number of observational studies.

With the help of observational schedules it has been possible to compare the environment in a pre-school unit as experienced by children with special needs and matched children not so identified. In this way it has been possible to study both the extent to which such children are 'integrated' into an ordinary pre-school setting or, if specially referred, receive the extra attention intended for them, and compare their environment with that of children placed in special units. The observation schedule developed by Robson for a study of children with special needs was amended and used effectively in a variety of studies of children from different ethnic backgrounds (Clark, Barr and Dewhirst, 1984). It was also used for their dissertations by a number of students, who were themselves teachers in pre-school units, with many children from different ethnic minority backgrounds. The studies provided these practitioners with insights which led them to question their own practice and to change the organisation of activities in their own settings. Details of how to use these schedules are given in Robson (1989).

The nature and extent of experiences relating to literacy and numeracy available to two- and three-year-old children in nurseries has been investigated using observational techniques by Munn and Schaffer (1993). They set out to identify the nurseries which were most effective in providing such opportunities for their 'disadvantaged young children'. They found that exposure to materials was not in itself sufficient, leading only to infrequent and fleeting contact. Social interaction with an adult was a crucial element.

Some researchers have used observation schedules to assess the range and duration of activities provided for and undertaken by young children in the reception class and beyond. Bennett and Kell (1989), for example, studied four-year-olds in reception class. Although play activities, they argue, can be high quality learning experiences, they found this was seldom the case. In many classes play was used as a 'filler' activity whose purpose was not made clear. The assumption seemed to be that any play was 'good' play. Their observations showed that, in many instances, well planned activities often failed in practice in these classrooms. Many teachers, while they made clear to children what to do, did not make clear to them the purpose of what they were doing. Thus judgments by the child, and sometimes subsequently by the teacher, of whether the task had been successful, did not necessarily relate to the planned purpose of the activity as stated to the researcher.

In a few studies children, already observed at the pre-school stage, have been followed into reception class [see Barrett (1986) who also observed the children at home]. This has made it possible to compare the learning opportunities provided for children in different settings. In the reception class, 'work' rather than 'play' became the aim; some children appeared to become more rather than less dependent; and for some children the level of work regarded as acceptable was on a lower level than they had achieved either at pre-school or at home. The organisation of the reception classroom and, in some, the presence of only one adult, meant that children had to acquire 'survival skills'. These studies show how important it is to plan the curriculum so that young children have challenge and continuity as they move from one class to another.

In an attempt to assess whether type of pre-school attended does have an effect on children's behaviour in the early stages of the primary school, Jowett and Sylva

(1986) compared the activities in which the children engaged, the complexity of these activities and the ways the children reacted to difficulties. The sample included children who had attended playgroups and others who had attended nursery classes or units. They found that children who had attended nursery class concentrated better, were more independent and were more inclined to approach teachers as resources for learning. Eagerness to learn and skill in seeking help when needed are both important attributes to cultivate in young children.

In a few studies the observation of selected children has continued beyond the reception class and their educational progress has been measured. Thus it has been possible to consider the effect on educational progress of different environments within the classroom, or the effects of different amounts of attention. Wells (1986) and his colleagues recorded children's language at home, then observed a selection of these children in their classrooms throughout the primary school, measuring their attainment and relating that to their classroom environments. Tizard and her colleagues, (1988), as part of their research into the relative progress of boys and girls of white and Afro-Caribbean origin in London, observed selected children in their classrooms over a three year period and assessed their attainment in reading, writing and mathematics. Both studies found marked differences in the appropriateness of the attention and curriculum coverage given to children of comparable attainment by their class teachers.

The evidence from the observational researches in pre-school units in the 1970s and 1980s challenged some of the firmly held beliefs of pre-school educators about the quality of play and the extent of dialogue between adults and children in pre-school settings. It also provided insights for practitioners on choice of activities and ways of organising these to make their pre-school settings more effective as enjoyable and stimulating learning environments for young children. Where the same children have been observed in pre-school, and again in primary school, the findings have challenged some of the assumptions of those who believe that education in primary school provides children with more demanding tasks and greater independence of thought than they could have been experiencing in the pre-school. Likewise, we now have evidence that, for many children, the home provides important educational opportunities that professional educators ignore at their peril. This is not the place to evaluate or even to summarise the findings of specific studies. As noted earlier in this chapter, what is important for practitioners is not so much the evidence from a single piece of research, but the insights which come from a growing body of evidence. The key references on which the views expressed in this chapter are based have been cited above and the reader interested in detailed evaluation of the main British studies of relevance to the education of children under five is referred to Chapters 6, 7 and 8 of Clark (1988) and to Clark (1989).

Recording dialogue in early education

The importance of language in young children's development is well recognised. Observational schedules do enable a researcher to obtain *quantitative* information on talk in the pre-schools, on length of conversations, on turn-taking by child and adult, perhaps even on numbers of questions asked by child and adult. What is not possible, even with note-taking during observations, is to make a full evaluation of the *quality* of the language interactions. In experimental settings, and in some contexts in the classroom, a sensitive microphone and a tape recorder may capture the quality of the dialogue between children or between adult and child. Two examples will be quoted, one from the pre-school and one from the infant school, of insights gained by practitioners using a tape recorder to capture, for later analysis, discussions between themselves and children.

The first example, which comes from the Oxford researches referred to earlier, was undertaken by Wood and his colleagues (1980). Interestingly, this aspect of the study was provoked by one of the practitioners in whose classroom observations had previously taken place, and who felt that, because the precise language was not recorded, the purpose behind the activities had not been captured. The recordings in this study were therefore made by the practitioners themselves and they were later able to study the recordings and gain insight into how particular children responded to their particular style of interaction. Lessons were learned about how certain styles of management in dialogue facilitated extended talk from the children, how some activities with a goal understood by the children could stimulate 'real' conversation between small groups of children as they attempted to solve a task, or communicate their discoveries with others. Some practitioners were able to modify their style of interaction as a consequence and to increase the length and continuity of their conversations with children. There is valuable material in the form of transcripts for group discussion during in-service training in the appendix to the book referred to above.

The second example of the use of tape recordings to improve dialogue in the classroom is from a book entitled *Wally's Stories* by Paley (1981), an infant class teacher in the United States. In her multi-ethnic classroom she initiated talk which she recorded about a number of topics which fascinated the children, such as where babies come from, whether Santa is black or white, what would happen if we all spoke the same language. By studying these recordings Paley gained insights into the children's thinking and was able to explore some of the issues with them again with greater awareness of their level of development than she would have had otherwise. She was thus able to use the children's fantasies to stimulate the level of thinking of which her five-year-olds were capable at that stage. She also used the material to discuss with slightly older children what they thought of the views of the younger children, and how they would have responded to similar topics.

The development of radio-microphones has made it possible to record language interactions in naturalistic pre-school settings and in the home where recordings with conventional microphones would not have been possible. In free play settings the voices of other children would have distorted the recordings, and the children's freedom would have had to be curtailed to keep them within range of the microphone. Recordings made with radio-microphones have opened up a whole new field since dialogue between children out of earshot of the adult has been recorded, as has language between parents and their children in the home, without the intrusion of a researcher. As long as recordings were confined to experimental settings, or were only undertaken when the talk was under the direction of a professional, it was tenable to assume that the conversations of young children, in the absence of an adult, would be more fragmented and of poorer quality. It was also assumed that the language of so-called 'disadvantaged' children in their homes would be more limited than at school and that their parents were likely to fail to provide them with the stimulus for extended discussion. Three well known studies which used radio-microphones, however, present evidence to give a rather different picture. Because their educational implications are so important, the reader is reminded of them here.

The study by Tizard and Hughes, which was initially published in a series of research articles, aroused controversy when it was summarised in popular version in a book entitled *Young Children Learning: talking and thinking at home and at school* (Tizard and Hughes, 1984). At that time nursery education was under grave threat, and some of the publicity surrounding that study suggested that, contrary to the belief of the professionals, even disadvantaged children gained qualitatively better language experiences at home than they received in the pre-school. For an evaluation and summary of that study the reader is referred to Clark (1988), Chapter 5.

The point which still needs to be stressed from the findings of that study is that professionals must not assume that the dialogue in which they engage with children in pre-schools is necessarily more extended or of higher quality than the dialogue children might experience at home. What is important for schools to recognise is that activities should be devised as a focus for the kind of dialogue which encourages 'real' communication, and that experiences which adults and children share are utilized to help less able children report on past events and project into the future. It is all too easy for the interchanges between adults and children to be brief and interrupted, to focus only on 'the here and now', or for adults to misunderstand the young child's attempts at communication.

Professionals have to face problems that the parent may not face in this connection as there are fewer shared experiences on which to call and far more young children clamouring for attention. Mothers in the study by Tizard and Hughes were in a totally different position: they were recorded at home when they were alone with their daughter in the afternoons; much shared experience could be taken for granted; much of the discussion was around joint activities in the home. Furthermore, questions which we as professionals use so much as our 'stock-in-trade', particularly with children who are shy and withdrawn, were found to result in minimum responses in the pre-school group. Enabling dialogue by adults, in which they contribute some of their own thoughts and experiences, combined with sparing use of questions, results in more extended contributions by even the less competent children. What Tizard and Hughes did not analyse was the language of the children in the nursery classes when in conversation with their peers. Some of that language might well have been stimulated by the activities and ideas provided by the adults.

In several studies in pre-school units in the West Midlands we used radio-microphones to record and analyse the dialogue not only between the adults and target children but also between children and their peers during play. We found that there was, on occasion, dialogue between children which was of a high quality and which had been stimulated by situations or topics introduced by the adults. However, we also found evidence similar to that of Tizard and Hughes of many limited and fragmented interchanges between adults and some children, often those in most need (Clark, Robson and Browning, 1982). In a further study we again used radio-microphones to provide samples of language in a number of settings, pre-school and reception class, with peers and with adults, to measure children's ability. Using the results of standardised tests along with assessments of their competence in English obtained in other situations, we were then able to identify the communication styles employed by adults which were most enabling to the children (Clark, Barr and Dewhirst, 1984).

In one novel setting we recorded the dialogue between young children in the reception class in groups of four, in the absence of an adult, and showed that even such young children, some of whom had a limited command of English, can engage in meaningful extended dialogue, with most children taking part. Stimulated by a number of what were for them 'intriguing' objects, such as torches, which they shared, children tried, for example, to make one of the torches work, and to use it with coloured materials to make patterns. In this kind of activity there was an impressively high level of discussion involving, in most groups, all of the children. The key was that the children saw purpose in the discussion and could support and demonstrate their meanings in action with the materials. Different qualities were added to the discussion when an adult joined the group, but the apparent competence of some of the children was also diminished as they then came to defer to the adult, a finding which was confirmed by the work of Coates (1985).

Settings such as these are valuable as stimulants for dialogue among children, as Coates herself had already found in her own reception classroom. She had frequently used such strategies in the past although she had not had the time or equipment to analyse just how effective they could be, even with children whose mother tongue was not English and who were still struggling to communicate. The adult has an important organisational role in selecting and varying the materials and planning the groupings. The attention and interventions of the adult can then be more selective and enabling for the children in greatest need. To provide stimulation and support for the shy, withdrawn and isolated child, the adult needs to be alert to the level of conversation at which that child can contribute. Then it is possible to provide one-to-one situations or small group situations which encourage and support communication.

The third study which pioneered the use of radio-microphones to record language in the home is that by Wells and his colleagues to which reference was made earlier. This equipment made it possible to record naturally occurring language over a period and to map children's language development during the pre-school years, identifying the situations which stimulated the richest language interchanges. Not only were the differences in the rate of the children's development analysed, it was also possible to relate these differences to their progress in later years in school and to identify the extent to which different classrooms provided learning environments suited to the needs of individual children. At the pre-school stage 'literacy related' activities, and in particular sharing of stories, was a rich source of dialogue. According to Wells (1986), these have a role in education which goes far beyond their contribution to literacy. Tizard and Hughes, in the study referred to above, also found that the longest conversations they recorded took place around books which the adult was reading aloud, or had just read aloud, or around joint activities in which adult and child engaged together.

Sophisticated radio-microphones may not be available other than within major research projects. However, the use of a tape recorder in some of these settings can provide valuable insights for the adult who can listen to inter-changes later and assess which were the more and less successful interventions. Robson (1983), following our studies, was able to use some of the transcripts from our recordings for in-service training of staff. Staff in early education can learn a great deal from discussions around recordings of themselves and their colleagues, in dialogue with particular groups of children, in one-to-one situa-tions with more precocious children, and with those who are shy or withdrawn.

Research evidence and practice in early education

Starting with Quality, the report of The Rumbold Com-mittee which considered the quality of educational provi-sion which should be offered to three- and four-year-olds, emphasises a number of the points made in this chapter and drawn from research (DES, 1990). In the section on 'Approaches to Learning' the importance of play is stressed as underlying a great deal of children's learning. For the play to achieve its potential, the report stresses the need for 'sensitive, knowledgeable and informed adult involvement and intervention', careful planning and organisation of the play settings, observation of children's activities to ensure 'planning for progression and continuity' and enough time for children to develop their play (para. 90, p. 11). The importance of 'talk' in children's learning, at home and in school, is stressed. For effective talk there is a need for access to adults who will stimulate and encourage conversation, adults who will offer views which help to 'elicit children's thoughtful participation' (para. 92, p. 11). Discussion between children in pairs and small groups can promote conversation and raise its complexity. The points made in the Rumbold Report are relevant to all early education, not only to that of children under the age of five. Similar points are made in the recently published report by HM Inspectors of Schools in Scotland, *Education of Children Under 5 in Scotland* (SOED, 1994).

Taken together, the development of sophisticated observational techniques and sensitive equipment to record dialogue in natural settings have made it possible to gain from research a wealth of evidence of value to those concerned to provide a quality learning environment for young children. The findings have challenged some of the firmly held convictions of those involved in early education about the educational potential for young children of some of the activities and settings we provide. They also reveal that many young children in the infant school, and at the pre-school stage, have powers of much greater concentration, independent activity and dialogue than we as adults have often given them credit for, provided the activities in which they are engaged are sufficiently challenging, and there is a 'real' purpose in communicating their discoveries.

All too often, in early education and elsewhere in education, we fall into the trap of plying children with questions, not for the sake of gaining information, but rather as a test of memory, where the person asking the question is already better informed than the child. Some of the more advanced children do play these 'games' to great effect; others do not or cannot, leading to an undervaluing of their knowledge and abilities. By the time they enter reception class there are already much wider differences not only in children's oral language, but also in their development towards literacy and numeracy. Research provides evidence on the range of such differences and on settings which appear to stimulate and foster such development.

Earlier in this chapter we outlined some of the dangers of administrative policies which mean that children in Britain may be entering primary schools as young as four or as old as five-and-a-half and are then faced with different forms of a 'national curriculum'. The dangers of over-stimulation on the one hand and lack of challenge on the other are obvious. Observational research, as we have indicated, gives some important clues about how children seem to learn best and in what kinds of settings. It is up to teachers to capitalise and build on that evidence if they are to provide educational experiences of real quality for our youngest children.

References

Barrett, G. (1986) *Starting School: an evaluation of the experience*. Final Report to AMMA. Norwich: University of East Anglia.

Bennett, N. and Kell, J. (1989) *A Good Start? Four-year olds in infant school*, Oxford: Blackwell Education.

Clark, M.M. (1988) *Children under Five: educational research and evidence*. Gordon and Breach (orders to PO Box 90, Reading, Berkshire RG1 8TJ).

Clark, M.M. (1989) *Understanding Research in Early Education*. Gordon and Breach (orders to PO Box 90, Reading, Berkshire RG1 8TJ).

Clark, M.M., Barr, J.E. and Dewhirst, W. (1984) *Early Education of Children with Communication Problems: particularly those from ethnic minorities*, Offset Pub. No. 3, Educational Review. Birmingham: University of Birmingham.

Clark, M.M., Robson, B. and Browning, M. (1982) *Pre-school Education and Children with Special Needs, Report of a research funded by DES 1979-81*. Educational Review, Birmingham: University of Birmingham.

Coates, E.A. (1985) An examination of the nature of young children's discussions, both in peer groups and with an adult, and the implications of these for the development of linguistic skills in the infant classroom, in Clark, M.M. (ed.) *Helping Communication in Early Education*, Occasional Pub. No. 11, Educational Review. Birmingham: University of Birmingham, Ch. 6, 49-59.

Department of Education and Science (1990) Starting with *Quality, the Report of the Committee of Enquiry into the Quality of the Educational Experience offered to 3- and 4-year olds* (The Rumbold Report). London: HMSO.

Hutt, S.J., Tyler, S., Hutt, C. and Christopherson, H. (1989) *Exploration and Learning: a natural history of the pre-school.* London: Routledge Education.

Jowett, S. and Sylva, K. (1986) Does kind of pre-school matter? *Educational Research*, 28 (1), 21-31.

Munn, P. and Schaffer, H.R. (1993) Literacy and numeracy events in social interactive contexts, *International Journal of Early Years Education*, 3 (1), 61-80.

Paley, V.J. (1981) *Wally's Stories.* Cambridge, Mass: Harvard University Press.

Robson, B. (1983) Encouraging dialogue in pre-school units: the role of the pink pamfer. *Educational Review*, 35 (2), 141-148.

Robson, B. (1989) *Pre-school Provision for Children with Special Needs.* London: Cassell.

Scottish Office Education Department (1993) *The Structure and Balance of the Curriculum 5-14 National Guidelines.* Edinburgh: HMSO.

Scottish Office Education Department (1994) *Education of Children under 5 in Scotland.* Edinburgh: HMSO.

Sylva, K., Roy, C. and Painter, M. (1980) *Childwatching at Playgroup and Nursery School.* London: Grant McIntyre.

Tizard, B., Blatchford, P, Burke, J., Farquhar, C. and Plewis, I. (1988) *Young Children at School in the Inner City.* Hove: Lawrence Erlbaum.

Tizard, B. and Hughes, M. (1984) *Young Children Learning: talking and thinking at home and at school.* London: Fontana.

Wells, G. (1986) *The Meaning Makers: children learning language and using language to learn.* New Hampshire: Heinemann Educational.

Wood, D., McMahon, L. and Cranstoun, Y. (1980) *Working with Under Fives.* London: Grant McIntyre.

CHAPTER 3

QUALITY FOR ADULTS: QUALITY FOR CHILDREN

Marion Flett and Gill Scott

Introduction

Involving parents in education can mean one of two things: the involvement of parents in their children's education or the involvement of adults who are parents in their own education. Both these meanings of the term have currency in present debates about early education (McGivney and Bateson, 1991; David, 1993). In this chapter we emphasise the importance of bringing quality issues into these debates. In particular we examine how the policy of 'bringing parents into education' has developed at these two levels in the early years sector in Scotland and how such a policy has the potential to improve services for young children and resources for families. We also, however, point to its limitations, as well as to the contradictions and problems encountered in attempting to develop services for young children which include their parents, and in attempting to develop child care alongside adult education. Can we provide quality for both children and adults on both models?

Involving Parents: involving mothers

There is little doubt that involving parents in their children's education has become a recognised strategy for improving children's early educational performance. The theory and practice of parents working together with educators to improve the quality of children's educational opportunities has developed considerably over the last thirty years. As Miriam David (1993) points out:

> One of the early objectives of social democratic policy makers was to reduce disparities between families on the basis of parental privilege or family poverty, in order to provide educational opportunities on the basis of academic merit .... The gradual consensus of social scientific opinion was that the best way to help children's educational progress and development was through a lack of dissonance between home and school. (p. 159)

It was by involving parents in their children's early education that policy-makers in the 1970s and 1980s hoped to reduce this dissonance, improve home-school relationships and achieve more 'effective parenting' (Bastiani, 1987).

A number of possible models of parent involvement in children's education developed over the period, often varying significantly in the implications they had for both the children themselves and their carers. Some involved only liaison and consultation with professionals, others were about 'partnership', others were about parent control. Some involved parents as volunteers in classrooms, others in developing parents' rooms in schools and under-fives groups, and some 'community nurseries' began to develop the idea of parents in a shared management role. In the new models of 'family centres' which evolved in the 1980s, the role for the parent was, however, very different, based as it was on the 'deficit model' of the family and the need for professional support. As we explore some of these models in our discussion, we need to ask: how do they relate in their different ways to the development of children, to the quality of home and school environments and to the range of interests (including those of their parents) served by child care and education?

Strategies for involving parents in their own education have had a much less clear line of development. National fears of a declining skill base, changes in women's expectations for their own lives (Sargent, 1991), and the opening up of opportunities in further and higher education through 'access' routes have all contributed to the increasing involvement of the parents of young children in their own education. Much of the debate concerning adult participation in education, however, has ignored the child care responsibilities of students and has taken the quality of child care environments for granted.

Nevertheless, the actual take-up of educational opportunities by parents with young children has led to increasing recognition of the need to integrate policies for meeting the needs of children with policies aimed at their parents (WEA, 1982; Hughes, 1991). It is increasingly acknowledged, for example, that parents of young children will themselves be disadvantaged in their learning unless there is good quality child care available. Many of the responses, to date, however, have been *ad hoc*: additional sessions at under-fives centres, after-school care, creches, and timetabling to accommodate children's school hours.

These new and different types of care, often outside the traditional nursery school, day nursery and playgroup models, have developed to meet the needs of women returners. There has, however, been serious concern over the quality of care that develops from these adult-led rather than child-led services. The concerns serve to highlight the varying and potential role of national and local child care policies in both children's development and equal opportunities strategies (Scott, 1989a; Cohen and Fraser, 1991).

As we examine some of these new types of child care it will be apparent that there are few generally agreed criteria of quality. Some attempts to clarify the criteria have occurred. For example, the European Commission Recommendation on Child Care (CEC, 1992) states:

> It is recommended that Member States should take and/or progressively encourage initiatives to enable women and men to reconcile their occupational, family and upbringing responsibilities arising from the care of children. (Article 1)

Furthermore it recommends initiatives including the provision of child care whilst parents are working, seeking work or following a course of education. Such child care, it recommends, should be affordable, combine reliable care from the point of view of safety with a general upbringing and pedagogical approach, and take into account the needs of both parents and children.

To evaluate how far initiatives in Scotland have achieved such aims we need to examine:

(i)   the level and adequacy of monitoring;
      (do we have sufficient information to make comparisons on quality between the different forms of provision?)
(ii) the effect of new forms of financing on accessibility and the type of environment offered to children;
      (are resources sufficient to provide for the needs of children?)
(iii) the ways in which child, parent and community interests inter-relate.
      (is the range of interests involved made explicit? what support is there from surrounding agencies to accommodate both children's and adults' interests?)

In any discussion of quality it is important to make explicit both the range of interests involved in child care and the underlying assumptions about the nature of children's and parents' needs. Much of the debate about 'parent involvement', for example, has been conceptualised as just that – *parent* involvement. In practice, of course, the debate has centred around *mothers'* availability and interests. The history of adult involvement in education has been dominated by the position of women in society and their role within the family. Because this has probably changed more in the last two decades than in any other comparable period, we have witnessed during this time an explosion in the growth of child care services, albeit largely underfunded, poorly resourced and accorded little official recognition or value. As we have already seen, we have also witnessed a parallel growth in initiatives designed to support parents, particularly to improve their 'parenting skills' and programmes designed to encourage adults to return to study. The vast majority of individuals involved, both as learners and as teachers in these often highly innovative programmes have been women. When men have appeared, they have most often been in positions of control and supervision rather than delivery and use.

This gender imbalance needs to be stressed at this point because it has an important bearing on how early childhood care and education is perceived: the involvement of 'parents' tends to assume the availability of women during the day; the roles of 'teacher' and 'mother' can often become confused; and the purposes of involvement are often vague. In the recently published Inspectorate Report (SOED, 1994) there is scant reference to gender issues in relation to staff, parents or children although it is acknowledged that few members of staff are male and there is concern expressed that this may 'perpetuate in the minds of children an outmoded concept of the roles of men and women in society' (p44). The concept may be outmoded, but the current reality is that it is still women who carry the major responsibility for the education of young children both as parents and as professionals. The marginalisation of child care as solely a women's issue combined with the lack of clarity of the purposes of 'parent involvement' highlights the way in which issues of 'quality' can become obscured by other contextual and ideological factors which often go unacknowledged.

The failure to acknowledge the gendered nature of parent involvement strategies has been tempered somewhat by recent pressures to have more male workers in the early years field (Ruxton, 1992), sometimes because of increasing numbers of unemployed males being available to take greater child care responsibilities. There has, however, been little shift towards the concept of the 'new man' as an equal participant in domestic and child care responsibilities (Morris, 1990; Phillips, 1990). In early childhood care and education it is still largely mothers who are involved, both in the home and at school (Hill, 1987; Walkerdine and Lucey, 1989; Moss, 1990). Parent involvement, in both concept and practice, remains largely gender blind. Equally in adult education, any discussion of child care issues has been centred on the educational needs of mothers.

This gender bias on both fronts affects, in fundamental ways, the quality of the educational experiences we offer both children and adults. With this in mind, we now look more closely at some of the common models of 'involvement' and examine their implications for the quality of what is offered.

Mothers in education: improving children's education

The development of different models of involvement can be traced to four areas of concern about home-school relationships which have emerged over the past three decades. The first focuses on how to improve the quality of children's educational performance by ensuring a closer match between the values of school and home. The second is that parents should have greater control over the quality of their own children's education through greater participation in their educational settings and through greater knowledge of how the system works. In early education, a third set of concerns has focused on the idea of improving mother – child relationships and hence both the quality of interaction in the home and the language development of the child. The fourth constellation of issues relates to the influence of parents on the quality of provision through their involvement in how that provision is shaped.

Improved home-school links: the involvement model

Building on research findings, educators now take for granted the idea of involving parents in both pre-school settings and in the early years of primary school. There has also been a growing acceptance that parents, particularly mothers, are the primary educators of their own young children. There are many examples of schools where the pre-school-primary transition for the children is handled well: links with parents are established at an early stage and continue in an appropriate way when children are settled in school; and the role of parents as educators is acknowledged and respected as being distinct from that of teachers as professionals (Edwards and Redfern, 1988). Such schools have a clear view of the purpose of the institution and its focus. Policies such as that of Grampian Regional Council on pre-school-primary transition (GRC, 1987) provide a supportive underpinning framework which encourages staff in both primary schools and pre-school settings in the formal and informal sectors to consider ways of involving parents.

Given the number of groups in which young children may be involved before they attend primary school, the contribution of mothers in terms of providing an essential element of continuity in the education and development of children needs to be recognised by both policy makers and practitioners (Watt and Flett, 1985; Watt, 1989; Hill, 1987). The Strathclyde *Partnership in Education Project* has demonstrated clearly the enhancement of children's educational performance where efforts were focused on working with parents as co-educators in the early years of the primary school (Hall, Kay and Struthers, 1992). This approach has now been further developed by Strathclyde Regional Council in its commitment to providing support for parents as an essential dimension of its Educational Development Service. There is little acknowledgement, however, that most of the parents who are involved are mothers. In many ways it has been easier to involve parents in nursery education settings because the service remains outwith the statutory sector. This is less true of social work provision, however, where attendance at a day care or family centre may be required as an alternative to children being taken into care.

The participation model

One example of staff-parent cooperation on this model is to be found at the Woodlands Nursery in Methil, Fife (Pugh *et al*, 1987), where a range of educational activities for both adults and younger children have been introduced on the basis of 'identifying needs and finding new ways of meeting them' (Twelvetrees, 1991), essentially a community development approach. The example of Woodlands raises some of the broader issues about the participation of mothers in the early education of their own young children. As Braun (1992) puts it,

> When a child goes to nursery or playgroup, or to a childminder, or creche, she will feel more confident and secure if she feels that her parents are confident

with the setting and if staff clearly respect her home and family. (p. 177)

The implications of this for early education providers are, however, still being worked out in practice. While the role of mothers as primary educators of their children is widely acknowledged, increasing numbers of women are not available to be present in early education settings and fulfil their educative role in other ways. Yet much of the rhetoric about parent involvement has assumed not only the availability but the desire of women to be involved in early learning groups. That assumption has been challenged by authors like Finch (1984), Ferri and Niblett (1977) and David (1986). The necessity of mothers to participate in this way in order to fulfil their educational role has been challenged particularly by Scarr and Dunn (1987), Tizard *et al* (1981) and New and David (1985).

All over Scotland there are examples of nurseries and schools where staff have made considerable efforts to develop the concept of a partnership with parents on the 'participation' model (Watt and Flett, 1985; SCAFA, 1987; Watt, 1990), but these efforts are often characterised by vagueness concerning the purpose of the exercise. Where, for example, professionals and para-professionals such as playgroup leaders regard it as their right to define the educational programme for children, parents remain in a subservient role in an essentially paternalistic relationship. Again, activities such as parents' meetings, book clubs, open days, social events and housekeeping tasks in classrooms or offices are somehow expected to exert influence on parents' knowledge and understanding of what early education is about. Too often

> working with parents sometimes assumes a life of its own, where all sorts of activities take place and their links to the welfare of children become tenuous. (Braun, 1992, p. 181)

The family dynamics model

There are settings, however, where involving mothers has a clear focus on efforts to support the dynamics of family relationships. The argument is couched in terms of improved interaction between mother and child, thus fostering the child's communication skills. This in turn, it is argued, will lead to increasing confidence and ability on the part of the child to benefit from the group learning experience. A major initiative to develop from this approach is that of home visiting schemes such as Homestart (Van der Eyken, 1982). Home visiting as one of a range of alternatives aimed at increased mother–child interaction has been included in many of the innovative pre-school projects in Scotland over the past two decades and is now seen as a useful mechanism for increasing contact with parents and families by both pre-school and school staff. The innovative approach taken by Greengables Nursery School in Edinburgh (McCail, 1981) has demonstrated the value of educational home visiting while raising many issues about how the needs of disadvantaged children are best served.

Home visiting programmes, however, illustrate many of the dilemmas facing educators. What should be the role of early education and care workers in trying to influence family interactions? Should they have a part to play in developing strategies for such intervention? Is this an effective means of support or does it reinforce the status of mothers as 'second class citizens'? In studies of teacher-child and mother-child interaction (Tizard et al, 1981; Tizard and Hughes, 1984) it has been found that, contrary to popular stereotype, children even from disadvantaged backgrounds often engage in a richer process of communication with their mothers at home than with staff in group settings. At the same time, however, there is an unspoken assumption that professionals know better than mothers and should be teaching them to be better educators. Walkerdine and Lucey (1989) suggest that, as professionals, our understanding of communication within the family is limited by our lack of knowledge of the social, economic and political frameworks in which working class families, particularly, live their lives. The implications of their argument indicate the need for change in professional attitudes and approaches if working class children are not to be further disadvantaged within the education system.

We find further examples of this dissonance between aims and practice in the development of family centres over the past two decades (Phelan, 1983; Holman, 1988; Cannan, 1992). The expansion in the number of such centres in Scotland, as in the UK as a whole, has often been at the expense of day care centres. Yet demand for child care has been growing rapidly as increasing numbers of women seek to rejoin the labour market. A clear conflict of interest results, therefore, when staff expect parents to be present to fulfil a family support function while parents are seeking child care to enable them to meet different responsibilities (Kirk, 1990). Again, while reference is normally made to 'parents' it is actually mothers who are expected to attend (Cannan, 1992). In his illuminating study of 'sharing child care' in Edinburgh, Malcolm Hill (1987) found that the majority of young children were left with carers other than the mother on a regular basis from babyhood onwards; that parents saw sharing care with others as a positive support for them in their role; and that they valued the educational as well as social benefits of group care for children of two and under. In her study of family centres, Cannan (1992) found that they provide a particular example of services based on ideologies about the role of women. Despite the rhetoric about *family* therapy and/or *family* support, the centres users were children and mothers. She highlights too a problem earlier identified by Van der Eyken (1985):

The language of social work refers to concepts of support and empowerment underpinning the programme
in family centres. Yet there can be little real sharing on
equal terms when attendance involves an element of
compulsion, however benign. (p. 27)

The empowerment model

In seeking to meet the needs of children and families
from more disadvantaged areas, the language of *empowerment* is now being increasingly heard (Barker, 1987;
Pantin, 1984). Yet often the rhetoric is not matched by the
evidence of practice on the ground (Chavez, 1989). Where
there is a commitment to genuine empowerment (Paz,
1990; Chetley, 1991; Cohen, 1991) there has to be a
recognition by professionals that an essential dimension
of the process is a sharing of control of the programme
with the participants (Pugh and De'Ath, 1989). This is not
an easy principle for professionals or others to put into
practice. However, many have tried to ensure that parents
are genuinely involved in the processes of management
and decision-making in relation to the broader issues of
educational provision, not simply those affecting their
own child.

The growth and development of the playgroup movement illustrates the opportunities and the dilemmas. Lack
of government support for the proposed expansion of
nursery education in the 1970s led to the expansion of the
voluntary nationwide movement offering an alternative to
state provision. Individual groups and the organisation as
a whole were both dependent for their survival on the
commitment and active participation of parents, largely
mothers. Increasingly, however, women began to demand
more space for themselves to pursue further education
and training or to take up employment. While the play-

group movement offered many women opportunities for experience of a power sharing model through active participation in the group and in management, it could not meet the needs of those whose primary interests lay elsewhere or whose family and work commitments did not allow for participation.

In more disadvantaged areas, funding provided through the government's Urban Programme or from charitable bodies allowed for innovative responses to the challenge of involving mothers on an empowerment model. The *Stepping Stones Projects* (Overton, 1981), for example, sought to develop a rather different model of participation, offering paid employment as an alternative to volunteer involvement. Other initiatives aimed to meet the challenge by making a clear distinction between involvement in management and decision-making and employment as child care workers. Examples of empowerment models include the *Young Families Now Project* (Flett, 1991), the *Powis Parent and Child Project* (Faulds, 1990) in Aberdeen and the *Craigroyston Under Fives Centre* in Edinburgh (Watt, 1988). There are others too numerous to mention individually, particularly those falling within the Strathclyde Region's community nurseries programme (Penn, 1990; Wilkinson *et al*, 1993).

The common strand characterising these initiatives has been the attempt to ensure that the voice of the local community is heard and appropriate responses made. The difficulties faced in obtaining long-term funding give some indication of how threatening the concept of empowerment can be when practice moves beyond rhetoric to demonstrate the implication of what greater control over their own lives by women in local communities can mean. There are, however, two problems which have political overtones. The first is that women who become empowered through community development programmes become a threat; the second is that women and young children generally have little political impact. As Paz (1990) says

The fact that the project was exclusively run by women, who in turn worked with women and children, served to diminish its impact on the life of the community as a whole. (p. 39)

In every educational setting for young children then, learning is enhanced by the quality of relationships between adults and children, among children, and among all the adults involved. We know that children do not thrive if their primary needs for affection and security are not met (Kellmer Pringle, 1980; Leach, 1979), and equally we observe how they flourish in caring, supportive settings. Creating a context of caring in which young children can grow and learn, building up confidence, enjoying challenge and stimulation in an atmosphere of warmth and safety, is what defines 'quality' early education. It cannot be achieved without all the adults involved sharing a recognition of their different roles and responsibilities. Good quality provision will seek to meet the needs of both children and mothers, as appropriate. It will never suggest that those needs are in opposition to one another.

Mothers involvement in adult education - new issues for the 1990s

In Scotland, concerns about improving child care in relation to parents' education have recently come from women themselves, those who provide training for employment and from educationists. This range of interested parties may be something new to those involved in providing early education and care but, as Balageur *et al* (1992) argue, the perspectives of parents, professionals and community are all important in examining the issue of quality.

Studies of parents with children under five throughout Scotland certainly indicate that mothers would consider taking up educational opportunities for themselves if there were good quality child care available to them (Cohen, 1989, Scott, 1989a; SCAFA , 1991). Cohen and Fraser (1991) suggest that

> the effects of the lack of child care provision on women's participation in further and higher education can be inferred from the drop in the proportion of students aged 20-30 (the prime childbearing years). (p. 40)

Women, moreover, are likely to cite the lack of good quality child care as a factor that prevents them returning to study at an early age (Gallagher*et al*, 1991)

This suggests that mothers' assessment of the quality of child care provision may be made partly in terms of its ability to allow all members of a household to benefit from educational opportunities. Indeed, a study of parents' preferences in relation to provision for their under - fives in Central Region (Scott and Culbert, 1992) showed that whilst access, cost and the relationship between child care and home are prime factors that parents use in judging a service, the availability and flexibility of places remains the major difficulty at each age level.

Others who are likely to judge the quality of child care provision partly in terms of its relationship to adult educational opportunities are employers, those who provide training for employment and educationists. Reasons for the interest of employers and training providers lie largely in the changed nature of the labour market and labour force. The interest of educational providers, in comparison, stems from the development of policies of social democratic reform to widen opportunities for women and fears of declining student numbers (David, 1993). As we shall see, however, criteria for evaluating child care for these parties has been more in terms of places made available than a close study of the environment provided for children.

Responses from the world of work

In the late 1980s employers in Scotland were keen to recruit and retain women with children and this led some to change employment and training policies (Steele and Peach, 1992). Other policy initiatives have come from government itself, such as child care allowances for lone parents on Employment Training schemes (Hughes, 1991).

As Hughes points out, however, whilst the Employment Training initiatives represent a shift away from traditional attitudes and assumptions, they have been characterised by a fairly limited acknowledgement of mothers' needs and a limitation to lone parents. In addition, the funding may contribute to overall child care provision but there is no guarantee of this, since it simply subsidises places and then leaves it up to the market to develop them. Judgment of the success of child care associated with employment training is therefore likely to be in terms of the number of adults taking up places.

An interesting question is whether the Local Enterprise Councils have adopted similar approaches to the related issues of child care and the education of mothers. A study of the LECs in Scotland (Training 2000, 1992) suggests this might be the case.

> At the time of the study the LECS had been established for less than one year but 12 out of 13 Scottish Enterprise LECS reported initiatives for women at least in the planning stage. (p. 56)

There is little evidence, however, of any such attention being given to the issue of quality in child care provision beyond an assessment of its availability. The use made by LECs of European funding for women's training and associated child care has still to be assessed.

Response from the European Commission

More wide ranging in their assessment of quality in child care are the providers of employment training funded by the European Commission. In 1990, for example, the Commission identified measures that were needed to help women into training. Within the framework of provision of the *New Opportunities for Women* initiative the Commission supports

> the creation of child care centres especially in zones of industrial concentration for the benefit of women; the operating costs of child care centres related to vocational training centres and the vocational training for the child care workers to raise their skills and consequently the quality of the service. (Commission of the European Communities, 1990, Com. (90) 449, 2.1, 3)

It is clear that whereas the Employment Training scheme tended to assess child care only in terms of what it allowed women to do, the European Commission approach combines concerns about the potential of child care to improve the employment and training prospects of mothers with a concern to ensure that the quality of the supporting child care is also recognised.

Supporting this wider based assessment of child care is the reform in 1988 of the European Community's Structural Funds which aims to balance economic and social development throughout the Community. Training for women and associated child care are seen to contribute to a number of the objectives of the Structural Funds: promoting the development and structural adjustment of less developed regions; revitalising the regions seriously affected by industrial decline; and combating long term unemployment. Combined with the recommendation of the Commission's Child Care Network that member states should ensure good quality services for children up to the age of ten for all parents employed or in training, this has resulted in a push towards the integration of interrelated child care and employment/training policies (Cohen and Fraser, 1991). A guiding principle of such policies has been the development of a partnership between the different authorities responsible for vocational training, employment and equal oppporrunities. The result is that a number of projects in Scotland involving employers, employment trainers and European Commission funds, have included both capital building and staff costs for child care as well as training allowances for mothers (Training 2000, 1992). In contrast to Denmark, however, the percentage of women benefiting from such European Social Funds in the U.K. declined rather than expanded between 1986 and 1990 (Alexopoulou, 1991).

Responses from Education

Responses to the issues of child care from the changing world of adult education are relatively new. One study as recently as 1989, for example (Scott, 1989b), found that over one third of further and higher education providers in Scotland were only then considering providing child care places for their students, and a further third had developed child care provision on site for their students only during the previous three years.

Increasing commitment to widening access for mature students, considerable support from some local authorities and increasing knowledge of how to access funds and partners, has led to new and effective strategies for increasing provision, particularly for the under fives. Evidence of wide interest in the issue of child care to support adult education was present in a conference organised by Strathclyde Regional Council Education Committee in 1992 (Strathclyde Regional Council, 1992). There has, however, as yet been very little evaluation of the child care provision that has developed.

One of the reasons is that, as providers of adult education, the institutions now interested in child care for students do not have the skills to plan and evaluate the day-to-day curriculum content and management of early years services. Increasingly they have turned to the private sector for such skills and the local authority for guidelines and authorisation. Recent contact (McTavish, 1992) with seven educational institutions with child care on site showed that six had given the day-to-day management of the child care to private concerns. Quality issues thereafter became a matter between parents, the local authority and the providers unless the college were also a provider of child care training.

A similar picture of changing forms and evaluations of child care emerges when we turn to child care in community-based education activities. Sessional creches for adult learners are a common development when community groups such as mother and toddler groups try to organise, with community education departments, some educational sessions for mothers. Adult learners in secondary schools have also produced a demand for sessional child care. Such provision is often supported by local authorities: Strathclyde and Grampian Regional Councils, for example, have budgets for sessional creches to support adult classes. The demand, however, has also been met by the private and voluntary sectors, by short term funding through projects in the Urban Programme and by the organisation of sessions for adults to coincide with children attending mainstream provision in primary school, nursery, or playgroup.

Monitoring the changes

In all these new forms of provision, there appears to have been very little attempt to monitor or evaluate the changes. This is true for both the nature of the provision itself and for its effects on children or adults. Providers themselves as well as those associated with employment training and adult educators seem to have had little interest in evaluating what is happening.

The lack of a unified system of evaluation is perhaps understandable given the variety of new forms of provision. They vary in size, in sources of funding, in resources available to them, in the cost to parents, in the proportion of trained staff, in their integration with other providers and educational establishments and in their aims. Some are purely sessional, others are integrated into the structures of the wider provision.

Comparison of the different forms of provision is made even more difficult because the criteria for assessing quality vary. The general criteria of success in child care related to European Social Fund projects may, for example, stress 'outcomes' for parents; employment or movement into other forms of education or training. For many further education colleges success may mean ability to attract women students. For child care staff it may be related to stability of employment and the availability of staff development. For parents it may be related to their child's development and the quality of communication between staff and parent.

One study which has made some attempt to evaluate child care provision in relation to adult education is worth reporting here. Carried out in Strathclyde Region in 1993, it does not cover all the varieties of child care which have emerged within adult education and training, but it does serve to highlight the patchwork of reponses to quality from parents, child care workers and educationists, the major issues of financial and staffing vulnerability which are involved, as well as parent preferences for different forms of child care and education. The study (Scott *et al,* 1993) involved a survey of 140 parents of P1 and P7 children in six primary schools, interviews with five groups of parent/students and observation visits to seven sites of child care provision related to adult education.

A high level of interest in studying amongst a wide range of parents but a dissatisfaction with available child care were identified. Nearly half the mothers surveyed were keen to study either now or in the near future. Over two thirds of all parents surveyed expressed positive attitudes towards the capacity of educational opportunities to improve their own intellectual, social and employment opportunities, as well as increase their understanding of their children's education.

Parents' dissatisfaction with the child care available to support their studies was based on a number of features. The level of child care provision for parent learners was felt to be low and parent preferences for different patterns and forms of care differed considerably from those they were actually using. The care presently used was very varied and often involved more than one carer. Many students would prefer some extension and integration of care for older children in order to allow them to plan and manage their educational career as their children entered full time education, but found that most available care was for the under fives. Parents were often able to organise their studies around the school hours of their older children, but this invariably meant their own studies could only continue part-time and their second 'educational career' was consequently lengthened.

Child care workers and providers interviewed for the study stressed different issues to those of parents. All had experienced difficulty in establishing and maintaining a well resourced, well organised service which was small enough to be sensitive to the needs of parents and children and large enough to be economically viable. The frequent neglect of the needs of adult returners in any discussion of child care needs at neighbourhood level meant that few sources of advice or support for the development of appropriate care were available, funding was difficult, staff training and conditions were relatively poor, the overall planning of provision and curriculum for children was difficult and the potential costs for students were high. The result was that continuity of education and care was vulnerable for both adult and child. It did, however, appear that larger community nurseries, particularly where adult education users were combined with other users such as working mothers and where a variety of sources of funding were used, had the greatest potential to provide continuity, flexibility and a varied curriculum for children.

The findings of this small-scale study are likely to be repeated once more careful evaluation of services at a regional and national level occurs. We have shown that adult education and related child care in Scotland is varied, but because the development of child care related to adult education opportunities has seldom occurred within a coherent child care and education policy, the result for children remains relatively poor and isolated services. Budgets for such provision tend to be subject to regular annual review, are often seen as an experiment or luxury and suffer from continual vulnerability. In addition, current developments suggest that policy makers are not providing clear guidance or support for items such as training across the wide range of provision that is developing. The resulting provision for children, therefore, will continue to vary considerably in quality and their experiences of education and care are likely to remain fragmented, relatively poorly resourced and underdeveloped.

At present, however, there is insufficient monitoring and evaluation to know exactly what the effect of different sources of funding and organisation are likely to be. Whilst many of the changes and developments are welcomed by mothers and education providers since they do widen opportunities for women and children, there is little doubt that for both groups the present pattern is disappointing. The low resourcing of facilities and lack of integration between child care provision amongst the different providers of educational opportunities limits the possibility of planned and effective progression for both generations.

The way forward: a two generational approach

At first sight the two approaches to the idea of 'mothers in education' discussed here appear to be in considerable contrast. The underlying ideologies contrast sharply in their views of women's role. Strategies to involve parents in children's education assume women's availability and that women's development is intimately connected to that of their children. In contrast, adult education is increasingly based on the idea that women are actual or potential members of the labour force. It recognises that many potential students and trainees are parents but assumes implicitly that the needs of children are of minor concern. It is a challenge which adult education recognises must be faced if women are to become part of a trained labour force. But child care is not an area in which adult educators themselves claim expertise, nor is it one which is considered relevant in planning for male students.

In practice too, the approaches have very different consequences. A focus on the child/parent relationship may improve children's educational success but it may just as easily reduce educational opportunities for mothers. Parent involvement strategies have frequently required considerable effort from mothers both in terms of income and in terms of their time as volunteers working alongside teachers. On the other hand, a focus on students who are also parents has improved access to education for women, but the poorly resourced and uncoordinated child care leaves children short-changed.

The situation is not, however, quite as polarised as it may first appear. Many mothers who would not have returned to education have found their interest kindled by a positive partnership with their child's nursery or school. Many children who would not have had access to child care facilities (particularly before the age of three) have enjoyed an enrichment of their social and educational experiences. This suggests that the two approaches are not mutually exclusive. Indeed a strong argument can be made that a clear reappraisal of the connections between the two sectors of education could be productive for all involved. Parents are not uni-dimensional in their interests and concerns. They are often interested in education for two reasons: a desire to improve their labour market potential and a desire to help their children. An approach which develops partnerships between educational providers and parents could assist parents significantly in their attempts both to help their children and to gain access to what they feel to be relevant education for themselves (Flett, 1990). Both research and practice suggest that widening opportunities for mothers, whilst recognising the integrated nature of the needs of both mothers and children, can very effectively improve women's educational opportunities and household resources, as well as improve current and future levels of educational skills. In other words, what we are advocating is a two generational approach. Achieving the right balance within such an approach, of course, raises dilemmas, but we suggest four possible ways forward.

First, careful monitoring of the nature and extent of provision is a vital element in assessing quality. The common *ad hoc* responses to lack of facilities has meant the rapid expansion of certain services such as crèches and childminding. As yet we know little about the criteria for quality in these settings because the pressures have been to increase service provision. We would certainly argue for retaining the principles of flexibility and responsiveness to need, but accept, as Peter Moss (1991) reminds us, that 'diversity does not mean choice'. An essential dimension of quality requires that a sufficient range and number of services are available to allow families to make real choices in relation to the separate and integrated needs of young children and their mothers. Whether children attend a crèche, day care centre, playgroup or nursery class, certain core needs remain the same. Crucial dimensions of choice for parents, however, remain affordability and congruence with employment and educational opportunities.

Second, if we accept that care and education are indivisible elements of all good quality early childhood programmes, then we can encourage evaluation of different services on their own terms rather than in comparison with other services with different emphases. This is important if we are to appreciate fully the value of each type of service and what it individually seeks to offer children and parents.

Third, coordination of both services and of training is clearly important. The danger of maintaining flexibility and diversity of provision is that it leads to fragmentation and dilution of services rather than extension of flexibility and choice. Current policy encourages local authorities to adopt an enabling rather than service provider role. This reinforces the uneasy mix in public service provision of child care, on the one hand, now virtually reduced to a minimalist service for children at risk or in need, and nursery education, on the other, the most expensive service to provide yet often the cheapest to access. Day care is now provided largely by the private and voluntary sector. There is an important role for local authorities in terms of coordination of both provision and support services. First steps have been taken in relation to the development of information services, training and support with the publication of the reviews of services for children under eight in every region as required by the Children Act (1989). Implicit in many of these reports is the acknowledgement that local authorities will need to work with the private and voluntary sectors to secure adequate resources for training to enhance the quality of care on offer.

Fourth, an overarching strategy to improve the quality of early childhood care and education is the development of community child care policies. Local authorities may not be able to act as direct providers, but they can put in place an underpinning structural framework of support for services. This implies the distribution of resources across all services to meet requirements as appropriate and with weighting given to those in greatest need. Tailoring services to the needs of local communities allows for the retention of the principles of responsiveness, adaptability and flexibility while ensuring a more coherent pattern of provision to meet the range of diverse needs.

Without greater emphasis on community-based provision, adequately resourced and supported by underpinning structural frameworks, the present *ad hoc* system will continue to be unsatisfactory. Brown and Tait (1992) refer to the ability of mothers in low income families to work 'small miracles' in attempting to piece together the jigsaw of child care provision required to support their working lives. In this chapter we have highlighted the fact that services for young children and their mothers in Scotland today are often of high quality in spite of the lack of support and sometimes against all odds. Yet we are aware, as are providers and users of the services, that the needs of children, particularly the most vulnerable children, are often poorly served by the current patchwork of provision. Unless we can develop better means of utilising our knowledge and experience of two generational approaches in education, then family inequalities will be reinforced and gender inequalities will increase. Most important of all, however, we will not fulfil our aims in terms of providing the best quality service to children in these vital early years.

References

Alexopoulou, C. (1991) What the European Social Fund does for Women *in Social Europe 3/91 Equal Opportunities for women and men*. Brussels: Commission of the European Communities.

Balageur, I., Mestres, J. and Penn, H. (1991) *Quality in Services for Young Children*. Brussels: Commission of the European Communities.

Barker, W. (1987) *Early Childhood Care and Education: the challenge*. The Hague: Bernard van Leer Foundation.

Bastiani, J. (ed.) (1987) *Perspectives on Home School Relations, Vol 1, Parents and Teachers* . Windsor: NFER- Nelson.

Borders Regional Council/SCAFA (1991) *Family Matters: a report of child care and employment and training in the Borders*. Edinburgh: Borders Regional Council/Scottish Child and Family Alliance.

Braun, D. (1992) Working with Parents, *in* Pugh, G. (ed.) *Contemporary Issues in the Early Years: working collaboratively for children*. London: Chapman/ National Children's Bureau.

Brown, U. and Tait, L. (1992) *Working Miracles: experiences of jobs and child care.* Glasgow: Scottish Low Pay Unit.

Cannan, C. (1992) *Changing Families, Changing Welfare*. Hemel Hempstead: Harvester Wheatsheaf.

Chavez, M. (1991) *Risk Factors and the Process of Empowerment, Studies and Evaluation Papers No 1*. The Hague: Bernard van Leer Foundation.

Chetley, A. (1990) *The Power to Change*. The Hague: Bernard van Leer Foundation.

Cohen, B. (1989) *Developing Nurseries in Glasgow: employers in partnership nurseries initiative.* Glasgow: Scottish Development Agency.

Cohen, B. and Fraser, N. (1991) *Child Care in a Modern Welfare System: towards a new policy*. London: Institute for Public Policy Research.

Cohen, R. (1991) *Shaping Tomorrow*. The Hague: Bernard van Leer Foundation.

Commission of the European Communities (1990) *Equal Opportunities For Men And Women: The Third Medium Term Community Action Programme*, 1991 - 1995, Com (90) 449, 2.1,3, Brussels: CEC.

Commission of the European Communities (1992) *Council Recommendation on Child care*. 31 March 1992. 92/241/EEC.

David, M. (1986) Teaching family matters, *British Journal of Sociology of Education,* 7, (1), 35-57.

David, M. (1993) *Parents, Gender and Education Reform*. Cambridge: Polity.

Edwards, V. and Redfern, A. (1988) *At Home in School: parent participation in primary education.* London: Routledge.

Faulds, F. (1990) The Powis Parent and Child Project, *The Scottish Child,* October/November 22-23.

Ferri, E. and Niblett, R. (1977) *Disadvantaged Families and Playgroups.* Slough: National Foundation for Educational Research.

Finch, J. (1984) The deceipt of self help: pre-school playgroups and working class mothers, *Journal of Social Policy,* 13, (1), 1-20.

Flett, M. (1990) Women in transition: gender and power, *Journal of Community Education,* 8, (4), 8-13.

Flett, M. (1991) *Education for Mothers and Children: a contribution to community development.* University of Aberdeen: Unpublished PhD Thesis.

Gallacher J., Scott, G. and White, A. (1992) *Scottish Wider Access Programme.* Glasgow: Glasgow Caledonian University.

Grampian Regional Council (1987) *Report of the Working Party Regarding Pre-school/Primary Liaison.* Aberdeen: Grampian Regional Council.

Hall, S., Kay, I. and Struthers, S. (1992) *The Experience of Partnership in Education.* Dereham: Peter Francis Publishers.

Hill, M. (1987) *Sharing Care in Early Parenthood.* London: Routledge and Kegan Paul.

Holman, B (1988) *Putting Families First: prevention and child care.* Basingstoke: Macmillan/The Children's Society.

Hughes, M. (1991) Mothers' Help: Policy on the Education of Mothers, *Adults Learning,* 3, (2), 49-51.

Kellmer Pringle, M. (1980) *The Needs of Children.* London: Hutchison.

Kirk, R. (1990) *Parents and Their Perceptions of Family Centres in Tayside.* University of Stirling: Unpublished MSc Thesis.

Leach, P. (1979) *Who Cares? A New Deal for Mothers and Their Small Children.* Harmondsworth: Penguin.

McCail, G. (1981) *Mother Start.* Edinburgh: Scottish Council for Research in Education.

McGivney, V. and Bateson, E. (1991) Child care: the continuing debate, *Adults Learning* 2, (7), 203-204.

McTavish, L. (1992) Further Education College Creches, in *Child Care to Support Adult Education: the Strathclyde perspective:* Issue Papers. Glasgow: Workers Educational Association.

Morris, L. (1990) *The Workings of the Household.* Cambridge: Polity Press.

Moss, P. (1990) Work, family and the care of children: issues of equality and responsibility, *Children and Society,* 4, (2), 145-166.

Moss, P. (1991) Day Care for Young Children in the UK, in Moss, P. and Melhuish, E. C. (eds.) *Day Care for Young Children.* London: Routledge.

New, C. and David, M. (1985) *For the Children's Sake: making child care more than women's business.* Harmondsworth: Penguin.

Overton, J. (1981) *Stepping Stones Projects: the first three years, 1978 - 81.* Glasgow: The Scottish Pre-school Playgroups Association.

Pantin, G. (1984) *The Servol Village,* Bernard van Leer Foundation International Series on Education. Ypsillanti: High/Scope Press.

Paz, R. (1990) *Paths to Empowerment.* The Hague: Bernard van Leer Foundation.

Penn, H. (1990) *Under Fives: the view from Strathclyde.* Edinburgh: Scottish Academic Press.

Phelan, J. (1983) *Family Centres: a study.* London: The Children's Society.

Phillips, A. (1990) Sins of the Fathers, *The Guardian,* 18. 1. 90.

Pugh, G., Aplin, G., De'Ath, E. and Moxon, M. (1987) *Partnership in Action: working with parents in pre-school centres.* London: National Children's Bureau.

Pugh, G. and De'Ath, E. (1989) *Working Towards Partnership in the Early Years.* London: National Children's Bureau.

Ruxton, S. (1992) *What's he doing at the Family Centre? : The dilemmas of men who care for children,* London, National Children's Homes

Sargent, N. (1991) Learning and Leisure: a study of adult participation, in *Learning and its Implications.* Leicester: National Institute of Adult and Continuing Education.

SCAFA (1987) *Parents in Partnership,* Conference Report. Edinburgh: Scottish Child and Family Alliance/National Children's Bureau.

Scarr, S. and Dunn, J. (1987) *Mother Care, Other Care: The child care dilemma for women and children.* Harmondsworth: Penguin.

Scott, G. (1989a) *Families and Under Fives.* Glasgow: Strathclyde Regional Council

Scott, G. (1989b) *Child Care and Access: women and tertiary education in Scotland.* Edinburgh: Scottish Institute of Adult and Continuing Education.

Scott, G. and Culbert, J. (1992) *Consumer Preference Study: pre-fives parents, Central Region.* Glasgow: Glasgow Caledonian University/Central Regional Council.

Scott, G., Culbert, J. and Fee, J. (1993) *Child Care and Adult Education.* Glasgow: Glasgow Caledonian University/Strathclyde Adult Education and Child Care Group.

Scottish Office Education Department (1994) *Education of Children Under 5 in Scotland.* Edinburgh: The Scottish Office.

Steele, M. and Peach, J. (1992) *Recruitment and Retention of Women in Scotland* Occasional Paper 4. Glasgow: Department of Human Resources Management, University of Strathclyde.

Strathclyde Regional Council (1992) *Child Care to Support Adult Education: the Strathclyde perspective,* Issue Papers. Glasgow: Workers Educational Association.

Tizard, B., Mortimore, J. and Burchell, B. (1981) *Involving Parents in Nursery and Infant Schools.* London: Grant McIntyre.

Tizard, B. and Hughes, M. (1984) *Young Children Learning: talking and thinking at home and at school.* London: Fontana.

Training 2000 (1992) *Women's Access to Jobs and Skills in Scotland.* Glasgow: Scottish Enterprise.

Twelvetrees, A. (1991) *Community Work.* Basingstoke: Macmillan Education Limited.

Van der Eyken, W. (1982) *Home Start: a four year evaluation.* Leicester: Home Start Consultancy.

Van der Eyken, W. (1985) Working with Parents in Day Nurseries, *Partnership Papers 4, Sharing the Care of Children: partnership with parents.* London: National Children's Bureau.

Walkerdine, V. and Lucey, H. (1989) *Democracy in the Kitchen: regulating mothers and socialising daughters.* London: Virago.

Watt, J. (1988) *Evaluation in Action: a case study of an under-fives centre in Scotland.* The Hague: Bernard van Leer Foundation.

Watt, J. (1989) Community Education and Parent Involvement: a Partnership in Need of a Theory, *in* MacLeod, F. (ed.) *Parents and Schools: the contemporary challenge.* Lewes: The Falmer Press.

Watt, J. (1990) *Early Education: the current debate.* Edinburgh: Scottish Academic Press.

Watt, J. and Flett, M. (1985) *Continuity in Early Education: the role of parents.* Aberdeen: University of Aberdeen Department of Education (mimeo).

Wilkinson, J. E., Kelly, B. and Stephen, C. (1993) *Flagships: an evaluation of community nurseries in Strathclyde 1989 - 1992.* Glasgow: Glasgow University Department of Education.

Workers Educational Association (1982) *Adults in Classes.* Aberdeen: Workers Educational Association.

CHAPTER 4

LEARNING IN THE EARLY YEARS CURRICULUM

Wendy Dignan, Moira Morrison and Joyce Watt

Introduction

There can be no more powerful focus for the debate on educational quality than the school curriculum – the total range of learning opportunities which schools offer to children. Few today would deny the central importance of the home and community for young children's learning, but the school curriculum remains at the heart of what government, as well as most parents and professionals, see as the educational key to both national economic regeneration and individual fulfilment. The appropriate nature of that curriculum, of course, remains hotly disputed and the early years sector has certainly not stood apart from that debate. Many of the issues relating to the early years curriculum, as these had evolved to the late 1980s in Scotland, are outlined in an earlier volume in this series (Watt, 1990), and are addressed most recently in a report from the Scottish Office Education Department, *Education of Children Under 5 in Scotland* (SOED, 1994).

The publication of the final versions of the National Curriculum Guidelines 5-14, (commonly referred to as the ' 5-14 Guidelines') in June 1993 has, however, taken the debate to a new stage in Scotland, and while it would be premature to attempt any comprehensive analysis of the likely impact of the Guidelines on the early years curriculum as it has operated, no discussion of 'quality' in early education in the mid-1990s can ignore one of the most significant curricular developments in Scottish primary education this century (SOED, 1991a,b, c; 1992 a,b; 1993 a,b, c).

This chapter therefore begins by examining the values and principles which traditionally have underpinned nursery and early primary school practice in Scotland and their relationship with current learning theory. It then outlines some of the values and principles which seem to underpin the 5-14 Guidelines and discusses both their internal consistency and their compatibility with what has traditionally been seen as 'good practice'. The chapter ends by arguing that the key to progress through 5-14 Guidelines can only be in enabling teachers to operate within an environment which puts learners first.

It is important to note that this discussion does not address directly the relationship between out-of-school learning and learning in school, nor does it discuss the role of parents in the curriculum. We take the fundamental importance of both for granted and welcome the initiative now being taken by the Scottish Consultative Council on the Curriculum to examine them in the context of the 5-14 Guidelines. In the present chapter, however, we focus specifically on the curriculum as it operates in schools and on issues which have arisen for teachers and others as the Guidelines begin to be implemented.

Values and the early years curriculum

'Values permeate all educational activity ' (SCCC, 1992, p. 2) and our perception of quality in education is a measure of the extent to which our own values accord with its aims and processes and the extent to which these aims are achieved. What a society wants for itself and for its children must therefore underpin what and how it deems children should learn in its schools, even in the earliest stages. The school curriculum, therefore, reflects the values of its own society.

In a fascinating study of pre-schools in three cultures, China, Japan and the United States of America, Tobin *et al* (1989) provide us with some glimpses of how the culture of the pre-school reveals the values of the wider culture in which it is set. In one of a myriad of examples, they show how language and its purposes can be differently harnessed.

> In China, the emphasis in language development is on enunciation, diction, memorisation, self-confidence in speaking and performing...... Language in Japan is viewed less as a tool for self expression than as a medium for expressing group solidarity and shared social purpose. Americans, in contrast, view words as the key to promoting individuality, autonomy, problem-solving, friendship and cognitive development in children. (pp. 189-190)

British policy-makers in the 1990s, in common with those in other Western democracies, would probably claim that the values which underpin social policies for children put them and their welfare at the centre of all decisions which affect them. Children's rights, needs and entitlements are at the heart of the Convention on the Rights of the Child as adopted by the General Assembly of the United Nations in 1989; children's welfare is the paramount consideration of the wide-ranging Children Act (1989); and the well-known traditions of child-centred education are again reiterated in the Rumbold Report (DES, 1990) where under-fives education is seen

> ...... to start with the needs and characteristics of the child which must be assessed through observation and collaboration with parents. (para. 63)

The political rhetoric would then claim that children and their needs remain at the centre of general social and educational policies in Britain in the early 1990s although the practical reality may at times present a rather different picture. What remains at issue is how children's 'needs' are defined and who defines them. This is a point to which we shall return.

Principles of the child-centred curriculum

The principles on which the early years child-centred curriculum have been built are well documented (Bruce, 1991; Curtis, 1986; Hurst, 1991; Lally, 1991) and need only brief mention here. Seven are identified as having particular relevance to the present discussion.

First, education is about the whole child: how the child feels, grows, communicates, relates to others and thinks are not only of equal importance, they are, like 'care' and 'education' themselves, 'complementary and inseparable' (Rumbold Report, DES, 1990, para. 62).

Second, children learn best by being active and interactive: by exploring, probing and manipulating their environment and by interacting with their peers, older children and adults. Opportunities for learning through and with others are of critical importance.

Third, children are individuals who are shaped by a host of personal characteristics and experiences and who learn in different ways. Adults who work with young children need to put a high priority on observing their actions and interactions, assessing their learning and planning accordingly.

Observation is the foundation of education in the early years. (Hurst, 1991, p. 70)

Fourth, play is the main mechanism through which young children learn. They do learn in other ways (Moyles, 1989) but play has a unique integrating function which moulds children's learning in ways which are meaningful to them. Some forms of play perform a major role in helping children develop an understanding of the use of symbols and in experimenting with their own through the symbolic use of objects, language, systems and signs in 'pretend' play. Nourot and van Hoorn (1991) in their review of the literature on symbolic play claim that it is critical to the development of thinking, problem solving, creativity and imagination as well as literacy skills.

> Play may contribute to this ability (effective problem solving) in much the same way that adults talk through alternatives to problems they face. (p. 43)

Fifth, the child-centred early years curriculum, to allow for the individuality of each child, needs to be flexible within a recognised framework of general aims.

> ..... what is needed is a flexible framework from which a curriculum can be developed to suit the needs of individual children in a variety of settings. (Rumbold Report, DES, 1990, para. 64)

Sixth, it is now accepted that there may be major gaps between what and how children learn in school and what they learn in the home and community (Tizard and Hughes, 1984; Tizard *et al*, 1988). It is incumbent on teachers to be aware of children's out of school learning and, in collaboration with parents, build on it within the school setting.

Finally, education is a continuous process, not simply between school and out of school learning, but between one educational stage and the next. As far as possible, within the constraints set by bridging statutory and non-statutory systems, children's learning from the nursery to the primary stage should be part of a continuous process, built on the same values and the same processes adapted to meet the evolving needs of the developing child.

Learning strategies: control and ownership

These principles accord well with current theories of learning, particularly those of the 'constructivist' school. For the constructivist,

> ...... learning is a personal construction of knowledge. We do not know merely from being told: we learn from action and interaction – interaction with the material to be learned, with the teacher, with our peers and with ourselves. (Nisbet, 1993, p. 285)

It is in this 'interactive'way that we make our learning our own and, given appropriate conditions, gradually take personal responsibility for its management and control. One of those 'conditions' is the nature of the social setting in which learning takes place. The social setting in which the learner interacts with peers and teachers not only provides meaning and motivation but encourages, supports and provides feedback to encourage learners to persevere in their tasks. It will also, at its best, make it clear to learners that critical thought and independence in learning are valued (Resnick and Klopfer, 1989).

> 'The social setting may also function to motivate students... They receive social support even for particularly unsuccessful efforts. Through this process, students come to think of themselves as capable of engaging in independent thinking......' (Resnick, 1987, p. 41)

Learners will also begin to appreciate the satisfactions and power of effective learning:

> ...... cognitive or intellectual mastery is rewarding. It is particularly so when the learner recognises the cumulative power of learning, that learning one thing permits him to go on to something that before was out of reach and so on towards such perfection as one may reach. (Bruner, 1974, p. 473)

What the constructivists are saying, then, is that learning is at the heart of education: that learning is a personal activity in a social context in which learners act and interact within their environment (including their human environment) in order to construct their own personal meanings and knowledge. The long-term aim is for them to take responsibility for their own learning.

As we have seen, it sits very easily beside the traditional principles of child-centred/learner-centred early education . The significant question, however, is whether child-centred and constructivist learner-centred principles sit beside the recommendations of 5-14 Guidelines, and, given the power of the political context in which these Guidelines are set, whether the curriculum of early education, particularly in the primary years, will develop along learner-centred lines or will be channelled along a different kind of path.

National Curriculum Guidelines: the messages

It is not feasible to describe in detail in a short chapter the background and content of the 5-14 Guidelines for Scottish schools. For readers outwith the Scottish context, however, it is important to note several major differences from the National Curriculum south of the Border: the 5-14 Guidelines are not enshrined in law; testing to national standards is mandatory at each stage but timing is left to the professional judgment of teachers and only in English Language and Mathematics; Guidelines cover seven years of primary education and the first two years of secondary education; and the curricular areas identified are English Language (SOED, 1991a), Mathematics (SOED, 1991b), Environmental Studies (SOED, 1993a), Expressive Arts (SOED, 1992a), and Religious and Moral Education (SOED, 1992b). Additional documents have also been published on Personal and Social Development (SOED,

1993b) and on Assessment (SOED, 1991c). Overall structure is discussed in the document *The Structure and Balance of the Curriculum 5-14* (SOED, 1993c). All primary and secondary schools in Scotland are now implementing these curricular guidelines according to their own school development plan. What then are the main messages of the 5-14 Guidelines which might give us more insight into how easily they complement the traditional principles of early education? Are they based on the same values and expectations?

It has to be said that the 5-14 Guidelines seem to present mixed messages. At one level they are unambiguously based on a model of the curriculum which takes identifiable 'forms of knowledge' and therefore curricular areas for granted. This is a model heavily criticised by Blenkin and Kelly (1987) and others as highly inappropriate for young children. The arguments have already been outlined in Watt (1990). The language is also the language of tight structure and teacher control: 'targets', 'attainment outcomes', 'strands' and 'programmes of study' seem to dominate.

> Within the curriculum as a whole ...... knowledge must be carefully structured and promoted if pupils are to assimilate it, understand its significance and make sure of the relationship between one form of knowledge and another. (SOED, 1993c, p. 4)

Children as learners do not seem to figure high on the priority list. It is

> ...... the nature of the subject matter, the character and size of the class and the layout of the school and classrooms (which) are all matters to be taken into account in determining the method appropriate to a particular activity. (SOED, 1993c, p. 20)

The document on Environmental Studies (SOED, 1993a, p. 6) does argue, however, that the separation of the 5-14 curriculum into five 'areas' should not obscure the links and common ground between them. This document, more than any of the others, highlights the importance of 'process' in education and the integration of knowledge through an 'action-based' curriculum. Investigating, observing, refining, describing, interpreting, evaluating, presenting and planning are the basis of all learning, and one of the main aims of the curriculum must be to develop

> the capacity for independent thought through enquiry, problem solving, information handling and reasoning. (SOED, 1993a, p. 3)

The 5-14 Guidelines on Assessment also provide mixed messages. On the one hand, they clearly, and unsurprisingly, use the language of 'attainment outcomes', 'levels', and 'testing' and are achievement-oriented. On the other, they argue for assessment to be seen as an integral part of learning and teaching on a daily basis and as a broad process which covers planning, teaching, recording, reporting and evaluating. Assessment is to be based on what pupils say and do as well as what they write and on observation of how they go about their tasks and activities. Its purpose is to promote learning and encourage learners:

> ...... assessment should develop and reinforce pupils' confidence and enthusiasm as learners, encouraging them to face new challenges. (SOED, 1991c, p. 12)

The quality of assessment is dependent on the quality of the context in which it is set and on the insights of the people responsible for it.

Interestingly, however, it is mainly left to the document on Personal and Social Development (SOED, 1993b) to argue the main case for learners being at the heart of education. It is envisaged that schools will help pupils

> ...... develop skills in working independently and take responsibility for their own learning (p. 3)

and through the development of self-awareness they will

> begin to have views of their own aptitudes and abilities,
> search for evidence about personal performance,
> recognise that developing self-awareness may lead to an
> increase in self control and
> recognise that making mistakes can provide opportuni-
> ties for learning. (p. 8)

All these last points are potentially constructivist in their orientation and in their emphasis on the learner.

What seems to emerge from the 5-14 Guidelines is a range of aims and values for the school curriculum which are often inconsistent and, at least for young children, incompatible in the processes they infer. Can a curriculum for young children which values 'attainment outcomes' and 'programmes of study' also value the child as a learner at its centre? We turn to the possible impact of the 5-14 Guidelines on first the nursery, and then the early primary school curriculum.

The 5-14 Guidelines and the nursery curriculum

The 5-14 Guidelines do not, of course, officially impinge on the curriculum of children in under-fives groups. The Rumbold Report (DES, 1990) was unequivocal on this point in the English context of a 'national curriculum':

> ...... there should be no suggestion of a National Cur-
> riculum for children of this age...... (para. 64)

Nevertheless, if continuity in early education is important, it is vital for both nursery and primary teachers to keep examining together what learning means for the child at each stage. For the moment we can do little more than speculate what the effects of the 5-14 Guidelines will be on the nursery curriculum. The dangers are obvious: that the under-fives curriculum should be modelled on the curriculum 'areas' identified within the Guidelines; that the 'attainment outcomes' of the early primary school become 'targets' for under-fives; that 'programmes of study' replace 'play' as the focus of the curriculum; in short that nursery education becomes a preparation for the primary school on a model of the curriculum which is totally inappropriate.

To date there is no evidence of this. In a recent national statement of the principles of early years education (SOED, 1994) it is emphasised:

> The model of a curriculum as a set of separate school subjects is inappropriate ...... for all children under 5. (para. 4.23)

At local authority level recent curriculum documents in the early years field produced by the two largest Scottish regions, still reflect strongly the values and principles which underpin the child-centred curriculum (Lothian Regional Council, 1992; Strathclyde Regional Council, 1994). Strathclyde emphasises its belief in the importance of a carefully conceived but child-centred curriculum for every kind of under-fives group; Lothian deliberately targets the three to eight age group as an integrated whole to emphasise the importance of curricular continuity, particularly between its nursery and primary schools. In neither document is there any evidence of a negative 'top-down' effect of the 5-14 Guidelines.

What is evident generally in Scotland is a new emphasis on assessment as an integral part of learning and teaching in nursery education and on 'profiling' as a joint activity between nursery staff and parents and shared between nursery and primary schools. The assessment and recording of children's learning has traditionally been a neglected field in the early years curriculum partly because of the narrow way it has often been conceived as something 'added on' and apart from the essential processes of teaching and learning. But assessment defined as an integral part of the learning process, which starts with the careful observation of children and through assessment leads to joint planning for their future learning, is at the heart of child-centred education. In constructivist terms, not only does it help adults plan a child's curriculum, it can also give children themselves, even at this stage, insight into their learning and help them both construct personal meaning from their experience and make the experience of learning their own.

While we have, as yet, no empirical evidence on the effects of the 5-14 Guidelines on the nursery curriculum in Scotland, some interesting evidence has emerged from south of the Border in relation to the National Curriculum.

In a questionnaire survey of early years educators in England, Sylva *et al* (1992) report what they call 'the worrying finding' that many early years educators (in both Education and Social Services nurseries) were including in their curriculum inappropriate 'targets' which reflected the aims of the National Curriculum in the early years of the primary school. This, the authors claim, was singularly inappropriate to the children's age group and 'incompatible with good nursery practice'. Teachers themselves feared the demise of play and were apprehensive about pressures from parents that children should be seen to aim for 'school-like achievements'.

On the other hand, teachers felt their assessment procedures and record-keeping had improved, that continuity between nursery and primary schools had strengthened because of joint in-service work, and the status of nursery education had also been enhanced because its contribution to children's learning in the early years had now been more explicitly recognised.

The 5-14 Guidelines and the early years of the primary school

The early years of the primary school are, however, of more immediate and more serious concern. We identify three general issues which raise, for us, serious doubts about whether the Guidelines can preserve the learner-centred traditions of early education: the need to observe and be aware of children as learners; the role of play; and what is meant by 'children as learners'.

The need to observe and be aware of children as learners

The knowledgeable and purposeful observation of children is central to the early years curriculum since:

> (Good) curriculum planning ...... depends on the quality of information about children. (Hurst, 1991 p. 73)

Skilled observation does not come easily: like any other skill, it demands guidance, feedback from others who are more experienced, cross-checking and practice. Its effectiveness in early education, as Lally (1991) argues, depends on the teacher's ability to

> observe each child as an individual and as part of a group;
> analyse and evaluate each observation;
> identify the significant parts of each observation; and use the information gained to inform an approach to a child. (p. 92)

The really skilled observer, as Drummond and Nutbrown (1992) claim, can use her observations to shape the child's present learning by identifying significant features and moments in it. Skilled observation can also give vital information on 'the learning yet to come'. Vygotsky (1962) suggests how informed observation can give adults insights into the development of children's learning by making them aware of the sometimes fine distinction between what children are capable of learning by themselves and what they are capable of learning with adult help. This 'scaffolding' of children's learning is the result of a process built on a cycle of observation, assessment and planning. It should involve collaboration among all the adults (including parents) who are responsible for promoting children's learning. At its best it will be done on a daily basis and in the presence of children.

While this is typical of the best nursery practice, it is less feasible for the P1 teacher normally working alone with a large group of children. Nevertheless, the teacher, committed to the principles of a child-centred curriculum, has to find strategies by which she can become aware of children as individual learners. Time must be built in for listening to children, responding to their interests – family and neighbourhood events for example, or ideas sparked by television programmes – observing them in their school settings, as well as being aware of how they are seen through their parents' eyes. This should be the basis of curriculum planning in the early years of the primary school as well as in the nursery.

The 5-14 Guidelines do, of course, insist on careful curriculum planning at every stage of the primary school and collaboration with other staff in that process is now taken for granted as good practice. But evidence to date would seem to suggest that two dangers are emerging. The first is an overemphasis on planning documents. There is certainly a need for some documentation, but pressures for teacher and school accountability in terms of school forward planning are in danger of focusing curriculum development on a planning process which takes a long time-scale, is remote from the immediate interests of children and encourages curriculum content to dominate. Planning documents may make teachers feel more secure in their control of what they do in classrooms; their danger, if conceived in 'accountability' terms, is that they encourage teachers to think of children as 'objects' or as 'projects' to be worked with and therefore to put their own control on children's learning.

The second danger is that, in the absence of carefully conceived strategies for the teacher to be aware of children as learners, she may come to 'observe' them only or largely through their learning 'products'. Illuminating though some of the clues may be,

> ......the products of children's learning are not always the best guides to what has been learned and the quality of that learning. (Moyles, 1989, p. 98)

Learning outcomes and products are important but they must not be seen in isolation from the processes and contexts of children's learning. From the teacher's perspective they are only one element in her total understanding of children's learning; from the children's perspective they are only meaningful if they are arrived at through their own routes. It is the teacher's professional task to be as aware as possible of children's personal routes to learning and to help them make their way along those routes.

The 5-14 Guidelines do not suggest anything specifically different to this but, with their implications for long-term planning, and their emphasis on 'programmes of study' and 'attainment outcomes' it is difficult to meet their demands and, at the same time, identify children's routes to learning.

The importance of play

As we have already indicated, the child-centred curriculum is based on the belief that one of the major routes to children's learning is through play. Again, the 5-14 Guidelines do not deny this but their specific reference to the value of play in education is minimal. We outline three main reasons why we think play for young children should have a much higher profile within the 5-14 Guidelines.

First, play can act as an integrating activity between different areas of the curriculum for young children: the child in the home corner can be involved in, for example, mathematical activities, language activities, personal and social relationships. Play is a child's route to the integration of different kinds of skills, knowledge and understanding. Since the 5-14 Guidelines advocate the integration of learning, play should be given a higher profile in the curriculum of the youngest children.

Second, play, as we have already seen, is one of the major opportunities children have to learn about symbolic meanings. The 5-14 Guidelines seem to assume that all children, by the time they reach the primary school, have reached the stage of understanding these symbolic meanings, but this is far from true. Many will not have had enough opportunity to explore the rich learning environment of, for example, blocks, make-believe games, books and stories along with other children and interested adults and most will need some extension of play well into the primary school. We ignore that at our peril.

Third, while play also provides opportunities for consolidating and practising skills and understanding, its major educational purpose is to *extend* children's learning.

> In play a child is always above his average age, above his daily behaviour; in play it is as if he were a head taller than himself. As in the focus of a magnifying glass, play contains all developmental tendencies in a condensed form; in play it is as if the child were trying to jump above the level of his usual behaviour. (Vygotsky, 1978, p. 102)

It is this function of play as a mechanism to stimulate, challenge and extend children's learning which is so often misunderstood. Too often it is seen as something trivial, something to wean children away from if their educational experiences are to be effective. In a newspaper interview on the possible expansion of nursery education a few years ago, Michael Forsyth, then Minister for Education in Scotland, suggested:

> It may be that there should be nursery school education rather than simply having the youngsters playing. (Quoted in *Scotland on Sunday*, 30.9.1990, p. 4)

There can be no more profound misunderstanding of the nature of play in education. Play has the potential to integrate the curriculum, and to provide opporunities for the symbolic understanding which underlies the development of knowledge in all curriculum areas. The quality of the teacher's responsiveness to the child is the crucial element in extending the child's learning.

Children as learners

It is not enough to claim that the early years curriculum should begin with children as learners. We must go beyond that and acknowledge that part of that concept is that children must 'learn how to learn' and eventually become responsible for and have control over their learning. What do we mean by this?

First, at the simplest level, children can take control of the organisation of their own learning: which activities they will choose, in what order, how long they will spend on each, and who they will work with. This seems to be the model which the Guidelines have in mind when they say:

> They (pupils) will discover how to take control of their own learning, to make choices and to work with others appreciating different points of view. (SOED, 1993c, p. 5)

This is in itself, however, a limited form of control.

Second, control may involve children beginning to analyse and articulate their own learning processes in terms of how they went about a task: for example, how they planned to build a bridge, what strategies they used and why, what succeeded or failed and how they might change the plan another time.

Third, children begin to take the major control of their learning when they begin to see themselves as learners: how well they have done; how they might learn from their mistakes; whether they have done better than last time; how good or bad they feel about their achievements and why.

These latter dimensions of children's learning, the more complex 'thinking' and 'feeling' aspects, have their roots in Vygotskian psychology where they are conceptualised as 'task involved' and 'self involved' inner speech respectively. Taken together, they form the core of 'ownership' of learning at any level. Those who learn to think about the processes of their own learning, and understand themselves as learners, come to control their own learning and, even as young children, begin progressively to be able to adapt a task or adapt themselves in order to achieve success. In Vygotskian terms:

> Together, self-involved and task-involved inner speech enable adaptive learning by allowing students to modify the task or the self and by enabling them to initiate and transform tasks. (Rohrkemper, 1989, p. 154)

To achieve this is probably a life-long task but it certainly has its roots in early childhood. Moreover, it may be that if children, who come to school highly motivated and eager to learn, find that 'control' is in the hands of teachers, they will fail to thrive as learners. Howard Gardner (1991) outlines three types and stages of learning: the 'intuitive learning' of the very young child; the 'traditional understanding' of most school learning which is based on

knowledge transmission from others; and the 'real understanding' of experts who have made knowledge their own
through appropriate learning experiences and through
the opportunity to reflect on their learning. Gardner
insists that few leave behind totally the intuitive understanding of the young child which, though serviceable
enough in its time is often immature, misleading or
fundamentally misconceived. He instances the primitive
understanding which many adults have of the laws of
physics, mathematics, literature and even morality:

> ...... the research of cognitive scientists demonstrates
> the surprising power and persistence of the young
> child's perception of the world. (p. 5)

Much of the failure of education, Gardner would argue, is
that it has failed to help children from the earliest stages
understand what learning is about or to control it in a
personal way.

 Are the 5-14 Guidelines likely to help or hinder this
process? We have already expressed our doubts about
whether they can help because of their lack of emphasis
on planning the curriculum according to the needs of
children and their lack of recognition of the importance
of play. At the heart of the problem is the statement:

> The curriculum for pupils 5-14 should provide a struc-
> ture and a programme of activities. (SOED, 1993c, p. 6)

and how that is to be interpreted.

 The danger for the youngest children is that any perception of the curriculum as a 'programme of activities'
based on 'subject matter' will carry with it its own language, encouraging children to define their learning in
artificial ways: 'finish your sums', 'put away your reading',
and most ironic of all, 'take out your Foundations of
Writing'. Such messages are not lost, even on the youngest
children. From the earliest stages of the primary school

they may, in the absence of any other evidence, begin to see the curriculum as a set of discrete tasks to be performed, and conform to what they see as the teacher's expectations of how they should be tackled. Inevitably,

> ...... there may be a strong risk that children abstract a set of work procedures rather than a conceptual understanding of the task. (Paris and Byrnes, 1989, p. 186)

At worst 'getting through the work' rather than 'learning' becomes the central focus. and the opportunity to 'learn how to learn' may be irretrievably lost. 'Getting through the work' also introduces a time dimension: an adult may, unthinkingly, cut across a child's play learning at a critical moment because the demands of a 'programme' or organisational constraints such as, ironically, 'playtime' take over and the control of the learning moves away from the child.

Children who, at home, or at nursery school have had the beginnings of control over their own learning on their own agenda at best will be confused, at worst will fail to learn if the agenda of the primary school not only belongs to the teacher but is expressed in teacher terms. '5-14' is an adult concept: 'mathematics', 'language' *etc* as areas of learning belong to the language of later stages. They are not how children conceptualise their learning. And children need to be able to conceptualise their learning if they are eventually to take control over it.

Again the 5-14 Guidelines do not deny this but neither do they make it explicit, certainly in the specific curriculum documents. As we have said, the document in which some of this kind of thinking is explicit is that which outlines thinking on personal and social development. If the principles of learning as set out there are liberally interpreted and fully integrated into the work of classrooms on a daily basis, then it is possible that the best of the old and the new may come together in an integrated curriculum based on learning. The key to that, however, has to be the professional learning of the teacher and the support which that is given.

Support for professional learning

If teachers are an important influence on ensuring quality in education then it is crucial that we recognise the kinds of qualities we want them to exemplify. Whatever else we look for, we must expect teachers to be responsive, reflective and critical, negotiating and challenging their own learning as they too aim for a process of self-direction and control. What we must recognise above all is that children will never develop as learners in the sense we have outlined unless the adults who support their learning take it for granted that they have to learn with them. Lally (1991) argues that:

> very young children need and deserve adults who are prepared to set out on a voyage of discovery with them. (p. 163)

The same kind of metaphor is used by Barsotti *et al* (1993):

> The work of day-care centres should be characterized by an exploring attitude. The expressions 'the exploring child' and 'the exploring teacher' reflect the belief that adults, as well as children, must be guided by an exploring attitude to work. (p. 11)

The critical point is that the exploration should be in some ways *mutual*. Teaching, according to Wells (1985), is about that mutual exploration: it is an attempt to negotiate 'shared meanings and understanding' and it can only be done in a learning environment which is flexible and interactive.

What then does this mean in terms of the 5-14 Guidelines? – given that they claim to provide opportunities for teachers to exercise professional judgment and expertise. (SOED, 1993c, p. 20)

First, it must mean that teachers are motivated to work in this way. Second, it must mean that teachers who focus the curriculum mainly on the transmission of knowledge do a disservice, not only to children, but to themselves.

> In programmes where the focus is on a one-way trans-mission of information, teachers find it difficult to advance their knowledge of child development because so much time has to be taken up with the content to be transmitted. (Athey, 1990, p. 30)

Third, and perhaps most important, teachers must them-selves truly understand not only the processes and context of learning, important though these are, but also the content on which it is based. Crucially, in early education, they have to be able to recognise that content as it emerges in the activities in which children are engaged, and har-ness it in educational ways. It is not enough simply for teachers to recognise what children are learning; to be effective, they must have a conceptual understanding of how that learning relates to different knowledge areas and to the curriculum as a whole. They have to be able to exploit the 'mathematics', the 'religious and moral' is-sues, the 'language' as they arise.

> ...... children's achievements need to be construed conceptually, not simply perceived. (Athey, 1990, p. 31)

Despite our reservations about an 'areas of knowledge' curriculum, it may be that the 5-14 Guidelines, if handled 'professionally', will help teachers in early education ena-bling them to recognise and respond to children's learn-ing more confidently and in more creative ways.

But this is a highly skilled professional task. Despite all that we have said about the importance of children and

adults taking control over their own learning, it is fundamental to our own thinking that no learner does this alone
at any stage; indeed successful learning will always to some
extent depend on others in a variety of ways. Donaldson
(1991), in her recent analysis of the evolution of 'human
minds' as they grow through a process of 'self transforma-
tion', makes the point:

> When we discuss the development of the human mind
> we are talking about processes of self-transformation:
> processes by which we turn ourselves into different
> human beings. However, in stressing self-transforma-
> tion, we should never forget that this is not a solitary
> effort. We are dependent in the most crucial ways on the
> help of others. And others may help or constrain us also.
> This is true from infancy onwards. (p. 20)

Certainly teachers are no exception to this. At this critical
stage in the development of the early years curriculum in
Scotland, they too need 'the help of others'; the mutual
support which can come from strong relationships with
parents and immediate colleagues. But they also need
specialist support, and here we have very serious reservations about what is happening in Scotland at the present
time. The specialist post of AHT (assistant headteacher,
early years) is fast disappearing in schools in many areas,
while the specialist qualifications in early years education
and the local authority advisory service are also under
threat.

Early years teachers need support both within the
school and from those outside who have a specialist
interest and experience in the field. This is not weakness:
what early years teachers traditionally have looked for is
not someone to lean on but someone to challenge them
and take their professional thinking and practice forward.
If the 5-14 Guidelines are to be implemented successfully
with learners at the centre, then that challenge and

support for both children and adults are vital. Where are they to come from in relation to teachers?

We return to where we began – to a recognition that what will determine the future of the curriculum of early education are the values which lie behind it and whose particular values come to dominate. We return to 'mixed messages' at three levels. First, we have the mixed messages which originate in a political ideology which sometimes uses the same language as 'learning to learn': 'individuality', 'ownership', 'personal control'. In the political context, however, it is set in a context of competition, market forces and entrepreneurial skill while in the learner-centred context it is embedded in the social interaction of learners. There are major differences in the underlying values.

Second, the mixed messages of the 5-14 Guidelines have already been alluded to many times: the contradictions arising from a curriculum based on programmes of activities and areas of knowledge which, at the same time, claims to aim for learner control; and the contradictions involved in arguing for teacher professionalism within a flexible curriculum framework which infers teacher accountability in terms of children's attainment levels.

Finally, however, we have to ask whether teachers themselves give mixed messages about their own values. Do they really believe in children as learners at the heart of the early years curriculum and in themselves as both learners and professional educators? That has to be the most significant question of all since, although the political climate is unpropitious, the 5-14 Guidelines, at least in their rhetoric, do not make it impossible to put learners back at the heart of the educational process. Mixed messages reflect mixed values. It remains to be seen which values and whose values will dominate the agenda of the early years curriculum and therefore how 'quality' comes to be interpreted as the National Curriculum Guidelines 5-14 are fully implemented and as society changes in the years ahead.

References

Athey, C. (1990) *Extending Thought in Young Children: a parent-teacher partnership*. London: Paul Chapman.

Barsotti, A., Dahlburg, G., Göthson, H and Asen Gunnar (1993) *Early Childhood Education in a Changing World – A Practice-Oriented Research Project*. Paper presented at the Third European Conference on the Quality of Early Childhood Education. Kriopigi, Greece, 1-3 September.

Blenkin, G. G. and Kelly, A. V. (eds.)(1987) *Early Childhood Education: a developmental curriculum*. London: Paul Chapman.

Bruce, T. (1991) *Time to Play in Early Childhood Education*. London: Hodder and Stoughton.

Bruner, J. (1974) Education as social invention, *in Beyond the Information Given: studies in the psychology of knowing*. London: Allen and Unwin.

Curtis, A. M. (1986) *A Curriculum for the Pre-School Child: Learning to Learn*. Windsor: NFER-Nelson.

Department of Education and Science (1990) *Starting with Quality: report of the Committee of Enquiry into the Educational Experiences offered to 3- and 4-year olds* (The Rumbold Report). London: HMSO.

Donaldson, M. (1991) *Human Minds: an exploration*. London: Allen and Unwin.

Drummond, M. J. and Nutbrown, C. (1992) Observing and assessing young children, *in* Pugh, G. (ed.) *Contemporary Issues in the Early Years: working collaboratively for children*. London: Paul Chapman and National Children's Bureau

Gardner, H. (1991) *The Unschooled Mind*. New York: Basic Books.

Hurst, V. (1991) *Planning for Early Learning: education in the first five years*. London: Paul Chapman.

Lally, M. (1991) *The Nursery Teacher in Action*. London: Paul Chapman.

Lothian Regional Council (1992) *A Curriculum for the Early Years*. Edinburgh: Lothian Regional Council, Department of Education.

Moyles, J. (1989) *Just Playing? The Role and Status of Play in Early Childhood Education*. Milton Keynes: Open University Press.

Nisbet, J. (1993) The thinking curriculum, *Educational Psychology* 13, (3 and 4), 281-290.

Nourot, P. M. and Van Hoorn, J. L. (1991) Symbolic play in pre-school and primary settings, *Young Children* 1, (1), 40-49.

Paris, S. G. and Byrnes, J. P. (1989) The constructivist approach to self-regulation in the classroom, *in* Zimmerman, B. J. and Schumk, D. H. (eds.) *Self-Regulated Learning and Academic Achievement: theory, research and practice*. New York, Tokyo, London: Springer-Verlag.

Resnick, L. B. (1987) *Education and Learning to Think*. Washington DC: National Academic Press.

Resnick, L. B. and Klopfer, L. E. (eds.)(1988) *Towards the Thinking Curriculum: Current Cognitive Research*. Alexandria, VA: Association for Supervision and Curriculum Development.

Rohrkemper, M. Mc. (1989) Self-regulated learning and academic achievement: a Vygotskian view, *in* Zimmerman, B. J. and Schumk, D. H. (eds.) *Self-Regulated Learning and Academic Achievement: theory, research and practice*. New York, Tokyo, London: Springer-Verlag.

Scottish Consultative Council on the Curriculum (1992) *Values in Education*. Dundee: Northern College.

Scottish Office Education Department (1991a) Curriculum and Assessment in Scotland: National Guidelines, *English Language 5-14*. Edinburgh: HMSO.

Scottish Office Education Department (1991b) Curriculum and Assessment in Scotland: National Guidelines, *Mathematics 5-14*. Edinburgh: HMSO.

Scottish Office Education Department (1991c) Curriculum and Assessment in Scotland: National Guidelines, *Assessment 5-14*. Edinburgh: HMSO.

Scottish Office Education Department (1992a) Curriculum and Assessment in Scotland: National Guidelines, *Expressive Arts 5-14*. Edinburgh: HMSO.

Scottish Office Education Department (1992b) Curriculum and Assessment in Scotland: National Guidelines, *Religious and Moral Development 5-14*. Edinburgh: HMSO.

Scottish Office Education Department (1993a) Curriculum and Assessment in Scotland: National Guidelines, *Environmental Studies 5-14*. Edinburgh: HMSO.

Scottish Office Education Department (1993b) Curriculum and Assessment in Scotland: National Guidelines, *Personal and Social Development 5-14*. Edinburgh: HMSO.

Scottish Office Education Department (1993c) Curriculum and Assessment in Scotland: National Guidlines, *The Structure and Balance of the Curriculum 5-14*. Edinburgh: HMSO.

Scottish Office Education Department (1994) *Education of Children Under 5 in Scotland*. Edinburgh: SOED.

Strathclyde Regional Council (1994) *Partners in Learning; 0-5 Curriculum Guidelines*. Glasgow: Strathclyde Regional Council.

Sylva, K., Blatchford, I., Johnson, S. (1992) The impact of the UK National Curriculum on pre-school practice, *International Journal of Early Childhood* 24 (1), 41-51.

Tizard, B. and Hughes, M. (1984) *Young Children Learning: talking and thinking at home and at school*. London: Fontana.

Tizard, B., Blatchford, P., Burke, J., Farquhar, C. and Plewis, I. (1988) *Young Children at School in the Inner City*. Hove: Erlbaum Associates.

Tobin, J., Wu, D. and Davidson, D. (1989) *Pre-school in Three Cultures*. New Haven and London: Yale University Press.

Vygotsky, L. (1962) *Thought and Language* Cambridge, Mass: Harvard University Press.

Vygotsky, L. (1978) *Mind in Society: the development of higher psychological processes*. Cambridge, Mass: Harvard University Press.

Watt, J. (1990) *Early Education: the current debate*. Edinburgh: Scottish Academic Press.

Wells, G. (1985) *Language Development in the Pre-school Years*. Cambridge: University Press.

CHAPTER 5

THE VOLUNTARY AND PUBLIC SECTORS: A PARTNERSHIP OF PARANOIAS ?

Esther Read

Introduction

It is not hard to understand why a sense of insecurity, and hence of paranoia, should permeate *all* sectors of early education. Research consistently testifies not only to the short-term worth of such provision but also to the long-term beneficial effects on those children who experience it (Osborn and Milbank, 1987). Despite this, consecutive governments continue to stop short of making the provision statutory (at least as far as the under-fives are concerned). Until recently, the standard question in relation to pre-school education was not, 'how good is it?' but simply, 'how available is it?'. The standard answer in 1992 was that 34.5% of all Scottish three and four year-olds were attending some form of local authority provision (Scottish Statistical Office, 1992). However, this is to ignore the whole host of agencies now offering an alternative service through the voluntary and private sectors, many of them, in the voluntary sector at least, with the aid of contributions from the public purse.

Two factors have led to an increased liaison between the public and voluntary sectors. Local authorities have found themselves faced with increasing demands from parents for improved pre-five services at the same time as their funding from central government has been progressively cut back. More recently, central government policy has decreed that as much non-statutory provision as possible should be 'contracted out', on the assumption that market forces will lead to greater efficiency and cost-effectiveness. This has obliged local authorities to adopt a more positive stance towards the voluntary sector. It has also established the need for accountability on both sides, pushing quality, at last, to the forefront of the discussion (The Rumbold Report, DES, 1990).

What are the organisations in the voluntary sector currently offering an alternative service in Scotland today? The list includes the Scottish Pre-School Play Association (SPPA), independent trusts such as Quarriers or the Aberlour Child Care Trust, the Association of Family Centres, the Scottish Society for the Prevention of Cruelty to Children (SSPCC), Barnardos and Save the Children. The intention of this chapter is to focus on the relationship between the public sector and the largest of these providers, the Scottish Pre-School Play Association.

The playgroup movement in Scotland was developed in the 1960s as a stopgap measure, a self-help approach by parents to meeting their young children's needs for group play until such time as the level of state nursery education could be improved. However, lessons learned in establishing playgroup provision soon changed that view. Parental involvement in the playroom, born of the necessity to keep costs down, led to parents feeling the need to inform themselves more about the nature of pre-school education. Training courses were established, run by parents for parents and for the playleaders whom they employed. Those unable or unwilling to attend courses were nevertheless involved in rota duty and had the opportunity to see in action the philosophy of child-centred, child-led education achieved through the medium of play. The result was that, for the first time, many parents felt able to carry on the child's education at home. Home became an extension of the playgroup and *vice versa*. This concept of genuine parental involvement in the management as well as the delivery of the provision is now central to SPPA's view of 'quality' in pre-school education.

Though it is difficult to be accurate about the exact level of playgroup provision in Scotland today as some groups offer five sessions a week and others only one or two and some children may attend more than one group, the figures for 1992 suggest that 49,733 children aged two to five were at that point attending their sessional groups (SPPA, 1992). The comparable figure for local authority nurseries was 46,992 (Scottish Statistical Office, 1992). A further 25,720 children are reported as attending toddler group with their parents.

This network of toddler groups, playgroups and under-fives groups parallels what is on offer from local authorities in more than numerical terms. The spread is country-wide and groups are open to all children, or at least to those whose parents can afford the fees. It is there, like local authority nursery education, to meet a general need and, like it, is offered, for the large part, on a part-time basis.

Small wonder, perhaps, that playgroups and nursery education have often been seen as in conflict or that those with an interest in increasing the amount of state provision have seen the existence of playgroups as an easy opt-out for politicians less than willing to fund a comprehensive pre-fives service. This is, however, to ignore the fact that consumers of the voluntary service are no less interested in the quality of what is on offer than they would be if they were availing themselves of a publicly-funded alternative. Indeed, as both providers *and* consumers, it is possible to argue that they are likely to have a far greater commitment to quality and far more understanding of what the concept implies.

Public funding comes to SPPA from a variety of sources. At national level, the Scottish Office provides funding towards a whole range of support services including training, publications, fieldwork and membership services. Individual groups, themselves autonomous organisations, tap into these services through a network of branch, divisional and regional committees of the Association each of which solicits funding from its respective local authority.

In the early days, the new Social Work Departments, established in 1968 at around the time the national play-group organisation was formed in Scotland, became the local authority agency chiefly responsible for administering grants though, in some instances, this role was shared with the community education sector of Education Departments. Social Work Departments were given responsibility for registering groups and for their general supervision but had no remit to assess the quality of their educational component. Their role was confined to inspecting premises, fixing the ratio of children to adults and checking on the health and any possible criminal records of those employed to work in groups.

The amount of financial support any group or region of the Association received depended on such factors as the priorities of the political party in power within the local authority and the attitudes of officials within a given administration. While much is often made of the high turnover of staff within the voluntary sector and the detrimental effect this may have on quality, less attention is paid to these other variables, yet in the absence of a national policy on under-fives services, their effects will be just as far-reaching. The point is crucial as it is the attitude underpinning the awarding of funds, rather than the overall amount, which ultimately makes a difference to the quality of what is on offer. Broadly, four models of the funding relationship exist. These range from control, through enabling, to co-operation and finally, to partnership.

Controlling and enabling

In 1992/93 Lothian Regional Council, in terms of

playgroup funding, was the highest awarding local authority in Scotland with £239,710 allocated for the funding of non-profit-making groups. Sums ranging from £700 to £2000 went directly to individual groups. The principle governing this funding was that playgroup provision should be available to all families in all parts of the Region at minimal cost to users and irrespective of ability to pay (Lothian Regional Council, 1993).

Grants were intended to cover property costs, insurance, SPPA membership and an allowance towards playleaders' salaries. Unfortunately, despite such generous across-the-board funding, the Council allowed only a small amount for the maintenance of the SPPA office which had to provide the support services needed to maintain quality. The conditions imposed on Lothian groups may well have been designed to ensure that all were 'equal' in financial terms but, in terms of quality, some were inevitably going to be more equal than others. In accordance with the criteria issued by the Council, fund-raising *was* 'appropriate for the benefit of the children' in direct terms, but central support services also have to be paid for and local groups are unlikely to be able to help. While parents may be willing to raise funds to maintain some sort of provision in their own community, it is difficult to motivate them to provide such umbrella services as training and fieldwork upon which quality control depends.

The money was being given to further the very specific aim of the Regional Council (the availability of *some* sort of provision for every pre-school child) rather than to improve the ability of a voluntary organisation to offer what *it* felt was an adequate service, and in that sense the issue was clearly one of control.

A contrasting scenario is found in Dumfries and Galloway where SPPA received a grant of £36,200 – £312 per group – in session 1992/93. As in Lothian Region, the local authority attached conditions. A 'special needs fund' was to be used to help with the transport of isolated children to playgroup and could be used to buy one-off items of equipment for handicapped children. Grants were available to playgroups to cover the costs of children attending in their final pre-school year where those children did not have a nursery place (though some children availed themselves of both kinds of provision). Money was also given to help groups paying high rental or heating bills.

Crucially, all money went directly to the regional association of SPPA which then became responsible for its administration and both the 'pre-school year grant' and the heating grant were available only to groups which were full members of the Association. The Council was thus implicitly endorsing the value of the support systems which the organisation offered and encouraging *all* groups to take advantage of them, enabling rather than controlling. The fact that money was also allocated specifically for fieldwork, training and resources, allowing the regional association to employ a regional fieldworker and implement a basic training course for playleaders, underlined the point.

Whether or not a local authority seeks to control or to enable is not just about establishing ownership of the service. In the absence of any local authority guidelines on quality (and until very recently there were none other than those applied solely to local authority nursery schools and classes), it is also a question of trust. Can 'unqualified' volunteers really be deemed capable of providing a quality service?

Of course, from the voluntary organisation's point of view, it is just as legitimate to turn such a question round. If educationists endorse the notion of parents as 'the prime educators of their children', what do they mean by that? Do they mean 'prime' in the sense of 'first' or 'prime' in the sense of 'most important'? And if the latter, what then is an appropriate role for the professional and how relevant is the training qualified staff currently receive? How well equipped are nursery nurses and teachers to work alongside or even in cooperation with parents? Are *they* enablers or controllers?

Cooperation and partnership

It seems clear that such questions are unlikely to be answered without some attempt at cross-referencing and a willingness on the part of both sectors to learn from each other. An early attempt to do both of these things came in 1979 with the setting up of what became known as *Link-up Groups* in Strathclyde Region (Strathclyde Regional Council, 1992). This followed a multi-disciplinary conference held in June of that year under the auspices of the Department of Adult and Continuing Education at Glasgow University. *Link-up Groups* were intended to be a forum of parents and professionals who would meet on a regular basis to share information and review educational and care provision for young children. It is possible to argue that, at least in part, this initiative laid the groundwork for the publication of the Member/Officer Report in Strathclyde Region (Strathclyde Regional Council, 1985) which led to the setting up of the Region's *Pre-Fives Unit,* now *Pre-Five Services.*

The Report took as its premise the notion that cooperation between all sectors offering pre-five care and education was not only possible but essential if a child's indivisible needs were to be met. Responsibility for care and education were all to be brought under the umbrella of the *Pre-Fives Unit.* More than that, in an effort to meet the child's needs, the unit would undertake to address the needs of the community from which that child came. This meant not only an amalgamation of the roles previously carried out separately by the Social Work and Education Departments but a commitment to working on an equal basis with other relevant agencies, including the voluntary sector. The lessons learned in that attempt, both on the part of the local authority and on the part of the voluntary sector, are salutary to all striving towards a similar ideal in other parts of the country (Penn, 1990).

Of the Report's many controversial proposals, perhaps the most controversial (and the one which most directly involved the voluntary sector) was the idea of 'community nurseries'. These were intended to be innovative in a number of ways, the most contentious proposal being that all staff (teachers and nursery nurses) would be employed on the same conditions of service, and that local experienced child carers, not necessarily professionally qualified, would also be employed.

One of the first pilot nurseries, the *Jigsaw Nursery* in South Strathkelvin, Dunbartonshire, was set up at the instigation of the voluntary sector. SPPA already had a playgroup in the location but had neither the financial nor legislative power to upgrade the premises nor acquire the necessary equipment. What it did have was the ability to empower the local community to lobby for the services it felt it required. Having done so successfully, the voluntary sector continued to be involved at all the consultative stages; yet once the project was up and running, it rapidly found itself sidelined, certainly insofar as the management of the facility was concerned.

Pugh and De'Ath (1989) define 'partnership' as

> a working relationship that is characterised by a shared sense of purpose, mutual respect and the willingness to negotiate. This implies a sharing of information, responsibility, skills, decision-making and accountability. (p. 68)

Can we say that a 'partnership' in these terms is developing between the public and the voluntary sector anywhere in Scotland?

Strathclyde has certainly gone a very long way in its willingness to listen to those parents represented by the voluntary sector and co-operate with them. As part of the pre-fives initiative, representatives of the voluntary sector were invited to be members of the pre-five sub-committee of the Region's Education Committee. However, they attend merely as advisers and have no vote. An *Early Years Voluntary Sector Forum* has also been set up to provide a formal link between the Region's Education Department, the Pre-five Committee and the voluntary sector. While consultation with the Forum and the sub-committee is extensive, it is consultation only after the initial policy-making discussions have taken place and hence stops short of true partnership in the sense outlined above. It seems a pity that the often innovative ideas of the voluntary sector should not be heard at as early a stage as possible.

Urban and rural needs

Nowhere is the need for cooperation and consequent joint decision-making more apparent than in areas of special need. The deprivation which exists in many of our inner cities has long been a subject of concern. Where the money for nursery provision has been available, it has often been poured into such areas as a way of 'rescuing' children from the poverty of their environment. Many voluntary agencies have also received funding for particular projects designed to relieve stress on parents and provide more opportunities for children to socialise, play and learn.

One example of this is the *Special Initiatives Project* in Strathclyde Region, run under the auspices of SPPA but supported financially by the Regional Council. Two workers are employed to facilitate a small number of groups. One is responsible for group development. This means far more than simply help with running the group: it also includes the personal development of the people who make it up. The worker offers help to parents in liaising with other agencies such as welfare rights organisations and encourages them to take up learning and training opportunities, beginning with SPPA training, but moving on to training on offer from community education departments of local authorities, local colleges and other agencies. Meantime the other worker concentrates on improving the quality of the play on offer to children.

At the start of the Project very few of the groups were SPPA members; now over 90% are. People who saw themselves as being alienated and disenfranchised by society are now learning to be accountable. What the Project highlights more than anything, however, is the distinction between the public sector's view of 'quality' and that traditionally associated with the voluntary sector.

Despite SPPA's insistence on parental involvement as a pre-requisite of quality, in one area of the Project, Haghill, it quickly became apparent that parents were so stressed they simply could not be expected to deliver what the Association's view of quality implied. A compromise was negotiated. Workers would be brought in to fulfil the parental role in the playroom for a limited period while the parents themselves would be offered 'respite care'. That did not, however, mean they could simply eschew responsibility for all that was going on. 'Courses' were offered to introduce them to what was being provided for their children and why, and gradually parents did feel sufficiently confident to resume their place in the playroom. Moreover, it was noticeable that they began to relate to their children in a different way; one good example was the way they took the trouble to help them dress up for Hallowe'en for the first time.

This insistence that a child's education cannot be separated from the context of the child's life generally changes our view not so much of what quality *is* as of how it can be *achieved.* As Bronfenbrenner (1976) put it:

> It is by taking as its focus neither the child nor the parent but the parent-child system that parent intervention apparently achieves its effectiveness and staying power. (p. 250)

Creating a quality educational environment is thus as much about motivating parents to be fully involved and responsible for their children's education as it is about laying down standards which they and their children must fit into. 'Quality', on this model, is always going to be an on-going process rather than a standard below which no one must be allowed to fall.

This has, of course, led to the accusation that 'standards' in playgroups are often poor: but 'poor' in terms of whose objectives? In a recent evaluation of the first three pilot community nurseries in Strathclyde Region it is interesting to note that, in one area of particular social deprivation, staff were unable to meet all their educational objectives in the initial stages because of problems relating to premises and the need to deal first with the social and behavioural problems of the children (Wilkinson *et al* , 1993). Given that playgroups are committed to working with parents and, of necessity, often have to operate in make-shift premises, it is possible that when comparisons are made between standards in local authority nurseries and playgroups, 'like' has simply not been compared with 'like'. This would apply whether the area was one of deprivation or not. It is important to recognise that before we assess the quality of any form of provision, the range of objectives the provision is aiming to meet must first be taken into account.

Despite the increasing involvement of voluntary organisations in special projects in urban areas, typically there are much higher levels of local authority provision in urban areas than in rural areas, and this has led to the use of the term 'rural disadvantage' in relation to under-fives provision. Although the term may be valid if applied strictly to the provision of 'nursery education', it is often hard for officials to understand how marginalised voluntary organisations feel at hearing their provision, long-established in rural areas, described in this way! A further problem is that, even where nursery education exists in a rural community, its catchment area tends to be very wide with resultant transport difficulties.

Grampian Region's solution to the problem of 'rural disadvantage' was to set up in 1990 'peripatetic nurseries', an idea now being either actively considered or implemented by a range of authorities, including Fife, Central, Highland, and Dumfries and Galloway. The system involves a number of nursery units being set up throughout the area and staffed most commonly on a three-sessions-a-week basis by teachers and nursery nurses who travel from unit to unit. Many of these units operate in communities where playgroups already exist and at least some share premises and equipment with existing playgroups. Some children attend both kinds of group. Is this, at last, the much-vaunted 'partnership' between the public and the voluntary sector?

In fact, the amount of consultation with the playgroups prior to nursery classes being set up has varied from place to place. Watt *et al* (1991) in an evaluation of Grampian's pilot scheme, found, unsurprisingly, that the idea seemed to work best where consultation had been most extensive. On the whole, where this kind of provision exists, it remains popular with parents who feel they are getting the best of both worlds and who welcome, above all, the opportunity for their children to enjoy up to five sessions a week, albeit that these sessions are offered by different agencies.

There are, of course, problems in this kind of 'partnership'. Children are being asked to adjust to two sets of provision which may vary not only in the content of the curriculum but also in the style of its delivery, and where continuity and stability are considered to be factors in quality provision, this is clearly of some concern. Nursery staff, too, in the initial evaluation by Watt *et al* (1991), found it difficult to relate to up to 60 sets of parents in a week and parents often felt they were not sufficiently involved in what was going on in the nursery. More recently, some parents have also been disappointed to discover that since the nursery provision was based on secondary school catchment areas, it still was not near enough to allow them to travel from their village and a new playgroup was formed as a result.

Problems also arise when local authorities offer nursery education on a priority basis to four-year-olds, a practice which, due to lack of resources, is common countrywide. There seems to be little thought given to the fact that this may make parent-run groups, in practice now relegated to catering for three-year-olds, harder to sustain. It is not just a question of reduced numbers; the objections go back to the notion of quality as a process rather than a neatly-packaged 'deliverable'. Where children have only one year in a playgroup, the time to develop the understanding and involvement of parents, necessary for the success of the concept of parent-managed provision, is also curtailed.

It will be argued, of course, that parents are not obliged to take up the nursery place when their child is four (and many don't). There is, it will be said, a 'choice'. However, as one parent noted in the *Family Matters* survey in Borders Region organised by the Scottish Child and Family Alliance (now Children in Scotland):

> Our playgroup is £1.20 per morning session, with fund-raising essential, whilst (school) nursery places are 50p per week – hardly an equal opportunity.
> (SCAFA, 1991, Section 4, para. 16)

'Choice' in that sense is an empty concept.

Taking a wider view, the policy also begins to alter subtly the ethos in which both the playgroup movement and pre-school education generally have operated hitherto. The philosophy has always been that the pre-school years are valuable in themselves and that during these years children's needs should be addressed on an individual basis and in terms of their developmental stage. In the public perception, however, the provision of nurseries primarily for four-year-olds suggests that what the provision is really about is preparing the child for school. Combine this narrow expectation with the pressures now being put on early education by the introduction of the National Curriculum Guidelines 5-14 (SOED, 1993), and the result is likely to be a narrowing down of what is on offer by all sectors to the detriment of quality. It seems no accident that playgroups are increasingly under pressure from parents to provide 'rising-fives' groups which are, in their own way, an attempt to match the pre-school year provided by nursery education.

Is there, however, an alternative way of improving the quality of provision in rural areas? It is possible that central government's *Under-Fives Initiative in Rural Areas* (*Hansard*, March 5th, 1992) has shown a different and perhaps more cost-effective way forward. This initiative was intended broadly to provide educational support for voluntary groups in rural areas and was planned on the assumption that for the foreseeable future voluntary provision would represent all provision in rural areas. Voluntary bodies were invited to tender for the £500,000 which would fund twelve projects, each to run for three years. Projects were intended to demonstrate to staff and parents ways of improving the quality of pre-five provision in rural communities, with particular emphasis on the educational component.

The projects, at the time of writing, are still on-going so it is difficult to assess how successful or otherwise they will be. In a recent article, Sue St. Joseph of Stewartry Branch of SPPA wrote of her committee's initial hostility to the project but then went on:

> We are completely converted ...... We now have some-one whose sole concern is 'play'. She's there to work with children, playleaders and parents in play groups; with committees and parents in information sessions; with Branch committee and members in training. Her being in post has freed other people to do other things and inspired us to aim even higher. The UFI Project has opened doors previously closed to us and there seems to be greater co-operation between Government depart-ments and other agencies concerned with pre-school children. (St. Joseph, 1994, p. 5)

It has to be admitted, however, that this is an SPPA volun-teer responding to an intiative being implemented by SPPA and employing workers familiar with the ethos of the organisation. In other areas where the funding went to a different organisation, there has been some resentment at the time needed for workers simply to familiarise them-selves with the situation when the existing SPPA fieldwork network, for the same resources, could have met the aims of the Project much more immediately and efficiently.

That said, it has to be remembered that the *Under Fives Initiative* is intended to give support not just to playgroups but to all those caring for pre-school children, including parents and childminders. It could be argued that, had the resources devoted to Grampian's peripatetic nursery project been similarly directed, then the result could have been improved quality of provision, not just for a few but for all.

The Children Act

It is, however, another Government measure, this time of a legislative nature, which is likely to have the greatest impact on the quality of pre-school provision, particularly in the voluntary sector. The Children Bill which received the Royal Assent in November 1989 and became the Children Act 1989 applies for the most part only to England and Wales. However, Part X, Section 19 of the Act contains some very important provisions which also apply in Scotland. These finally came into force on 14 October, 1991, replacing the Nurseries and Childminders Regulation Act , 1948.

The Act first of all defines the nature of services available to children under eight – childminding, day-care and education – and then goes on to indicate the ways in which local authorities are obliged to register, inspect and review such services. 'Sessional day care' is defined as day-care provided for children under eight for more than two hours but less than four hours per day in premises other than domestic premises, and hence most playgroups fall into this category (Statutory Instruments, 1991, No. 2129, *Children and Young Persons,* HMSO).

Local authorities were required to carry out reviews of their under-fives provision in consultation with health boards, voluntary organisations, employer interests, parents and other interested bodies and individuals. Most important of all, perhaps, Social Work and Education Departments were required to undertake the review as a joint exercise. This process has been an 'eye opener' for all concerned. As one voluntary sector representative commented:

The most amazing thing to me was the realisation that the various departments worked in such an insular way. Often a whole meeting would be taken up with Education, Community Education and Social Work all defending their own stance on issues and mostly all ignorant of what the other was doing. Quality was a classic example. Education were certain that they should state the guidelines while Social Work tried valiantly to de-

fend the policy they had put in place for the registration
process. (Personal communication)

The degree to which regions have involved the voluntary
sector continues to vary. Most have voluntary sector representatives providing input either as members of a specially
established 'voluntary sector forum' or as members of a
joint committee of all interested parties, including Social
Work and Education Department officials. From the point
of view of quality, it seems clear that the latter model will
work better. As Elfer (1991) has pointed out:

> In seeking to establish a quality service, the regulatory
> and developmental roles must be linked and need to be
> carried out in the context of a commonly worked out
> early years policy. (p. 14)

Much to the surprise of some, the voluntary sector has
regarded all these developments in a very positive light
since it seems that recognition is at last being given to the
educational component of its work. Indeed, the *Code of
Practice for SPPA Member Groups* (SPPA, 1990), was included
in the bibliography in the guidance to the Act originally
sent to local authorities by the Scottish Office.

However, the registration process has thrown up some
problems relating to premises, while even more problem-
atic has been the requirement for local authorities to
make some kind of assessment of the 'fitness' of those
providing care and education for young children.

The criteria go far beyond those set out by the previous
1948 Act. Authorities have been asked to consider such
things as the person's relevant qualifications and training,
relevant previous experience, ability to foster children's
development and learning, ability to provide warm and
consistent care, and knowledge of, and attitude to, multi-
cultural and equal opportunities issues. All of these things
are of course open to interpretation, and this remains one

of the main problems if the quality of provision is to be regarded as 'standard' across the country.

Training has thus become the focus for many joint initiatives. In Tayside, the under-eights training coordinator employed by the Region through its Education Department worked with volunteers and staff of the regional association of SPPA to develop a six session basic course for playleaders which became the minimum requirement for playleaders not otherwise qualified in early education or day care. In Fife, SPPA training is supported by regional staff and, as in Tayside, is open to other bodies and organisations where places are available. Similar developments are taking place throughout the country.

Scottish Vocational Qualifications, SVQs, which are assessed on the basis of a person's experience, might have offered one way forward in establishing across-the-board qualifications, except that access to voluntary organisations, childminders and others is being hindered by a lack of funding (SCVO, 1990). Not only is there a lack of people trained to do the assessments, there is also the problem of the cost to those applying to be assessed. Consortia are being set up in certain parts of the country, for example in Highland Region, where Highland SPPA are involved in the Inverness College Consortium, but progress looks like being painfully slow for the foreseeable future.

In the interim, SPPA is also developing its own national course for playleaders and a quality assurance pilot project is also underway. The latter involves the fieldworker visiting a group, observing the provision and then making recommendations on how it can be improved, based on the standards outlined in the SPPA *Code of Practice* (SPPA, 1990). These are discussed with a member of the committee and a playleader who then agree on a course of action.

These initiatives are, however, separate from the need to emphasise training which would help define standards and satisfy the inspection process demanded by The

Children Act. Such training is as necessary for the public sector as for the voluntary sector. As one local authority official responsible for the first round of registration put it, her only guideline for assessing quality at that stage was 'if the children looked happy'. With quality guidelines in place, the inspection process is likely to be much more stringent.

What the implementation of The Children Act has already demonstrated is that there is a tremendous willingness on the part of the voluntary sector to learn from the skills and expertise of the public sector, and a growing willingness on the part of the public sector, following the insights gained from closer cooperation, to learn more about flexible and innovative ways of working with parents. It would be good to finish on that optimistic note. Unfortunately, certain proposed developments threaten once more to put both standards and the amount of provision on offer in jeopardy, and consequently the development of a valid 'partnership' may again be under threat.

Future trends

The imminent reorganisation of local government in Scotland will pose a considerable threat to the future of the voluntary sector. As will have been noted, examples for this chapter have been largely based on the relationship between the current regions and the regional associations of SPPA.

The growth of these regional associations (many of which receive funding far in excess of that received by the central Scottish organisation) has, in many instances, been the major factor in facilitating the improvement in the quality of service on offer to SPPA groups. While funding of the national association by the Scottish Office has risen over the past ten years in overall terms, as a proportion of what is required that funding has fallen dramatically from 78% in 1981/82 to 52% in 1991/92. This has been linked to central government's policy of reducing substantially what is known as 'core funding' (funding which covers administrative costs or costs relating to central services) in favour of 'project funding' (funding for the delivery of particular services). This has had serious implications for an organisation which is not, on the whole, project-based but which is amongst the biggest providers of pre-school care in the country.

It is not simply that with the break-up of the regions, economies of scale may be lost and funding therefore may become less available. There is also the danger that much of the expertise, knowledge and good practice which has been so painstakingly built up over the past ten years will be lost. To date there has been no sign that central goverment is willing to cover the true costs of implementing plans which would avoid such an outcome of this transition. What is more, all this will be going on at the same time as plans for devolved school management could mean fewer resources going directly to the local authority (whatever that authority might be) and consequently less being available to fund an already limited nursery sector.

Yet another unknown will be the effect of the emerging 'contract culture'. Already several SPPA regions are finding that if they are in receipt of money over a given amount then they have to be far more accountable for how they use it. Many have been asked to enter into three-year agreements which have the advantage of making long-term planning easier, but, while this may be unobjectionable, it is but a short step to a situation where either local or national government seeks to use its purchasing power to drive through contracts which reflect the priorities of the party in power rather than the aims of the organisation.

Highland SPPA has faced up to this possibility by implementing a major restructuring of the organisation. The impetus for this was the recognition that, if the Association had to compete for business in the open market, then it had to be able to respond to the opportunities which presented themselves swiftly and effectively, something the previous committee structure did not necessarily allow for. More than that, in order to attract the available funding, they had to ensure that they presented a professional image, one where accurate costings for the service on offer and standards of accountability were built in.

The organisation is now therefore structured much more along business lines with four volunteer directors who meet as part of the wider regional committee five times a year in order to decide policy issues, but also meet separately on a monthly basis to take decisions necessary to the development of the 'business'. A business plan has been produced which both affirms the aims and objectives of the Association and seeks diversity of funding to help achieve them. The plan emphasises the point that 'value for money' does not mean 'cheap' and confirms the organisation's commitment to quality, reliability and validity of service.

Perhaps most significantly of all, Highland SPPA has also committed itself to taking part in the Investors in People programme, a standard instituted by Scottish Enterprise and the Highlands & Islands Enterprise and available to businesses keen to improve the quality and standards of their staff as a vital step on the road towards improving the quality of what the business has to offer. The scheme is administered under the auspices of the various Local Enterprise Companies. The standards implicit in the programme will, in Highland SPPA's case, be applied equally to volunteers. When we consider the 'makeshift and make-do' ethos in which the volunteer has traditionally operated, such an initiative clearly represents a radical departure.

But where does all of this leave the voluntary ethos? Will it deter those volunteers to whom the very lack of 'professionalism' was the attraction of the work? Will it lead, as Ann Coffey MP has suggested, to a 'publicly-run voluntary service, comprised of agencies that provide services'? (NCVO, 1993, p. 10).

One of the few negative experiences of the introduction of The Children Act was the tendency of some authorities, under pressure to complete the registration process in a very short timescale, to ask that voluntary sector representatives 'report back' on groups which they deemed unsatisfactory. Since the representatives saw their role as assisting in the process of quality rather than policing it, the request was refused but the fact that it was made highlights the dangers.

Conclusion

In summary, the past decade has seen many genuine attempts to improve the quality of pre-school provision through a closer working relationship between the public and voluntary sectors. It should not go unnoticed, however, that the most successful initiatives have been those which, like the development of the Strathclyde Pre-Fives Unit and the processes set in motion by the implementation of The Children Act, have come closest to accepting the voluntary sector as a full and equal partner in the development and delivery of services.

My grateful thanks must go to all my SPPA colleagues who so generously gave of their time and expertise to provide the information on which this chapter is based.

References

Bronfenbrenner, U. (1976) Is Early Education Effective? Facts and Principles of Early Intervention: a summary, *in* Clarke A. M. and Clarke, A. D. B. *Early Experience Myth and Evidence.* London: Open Books.

Department of Education and Science (1990) *Starting with Quality. The Report of the Committee of Enquiry into the Quality of Educational Experience Offered to 3 and 4 year-olds* (The Rumbold Report). London: HMSO.

Elfer, P. (1991) *Their Need - Our Future: ensuring standards in the care of young children.* London: National Children's Bureau.

Lothian Regional Council (1993) *Criteria for Grant Aid to Playgroups*. Report by the Director of Social Work No. 054, Appendix 1. Edinburgh: Lothian Regional Council.

National Council of Voluntary Organisations (1993) *NCVO News*. July/August.

Osborn, A. F. and Milbank, J. E. (1987) *The Effects of Early Education.* Oxford: Clarendon Press.

Penn, H. (1990) *Under Fives: The view from Strathclyde.* Professional Issues in Education 10, Edinburgh: Scottish Academic Press.

Pugh, G. and De'Ath, E. (1989) *Working towards Partnership in the Early Years.* London: National Children's Bureau.

St Joseph, S. (1994) Under-Fives in Rural Areas: *Parent to Parent. Journal of the Scottish Pre-school Play* Association, No. 10, February.

Scottish Child and Family Alliance (1991) *Family Matters: A report of a survey of child-care and employment and training in Borders Region.* Edinburgh: SCAFA.

Scottish Council of Voluntary Organisations (1990) *Passports of Excellence.* Edinburgh: SCVO.

Scottish Office Education Department (1993) *The Structure and Balance of the Curriculum 5-14.* Edinburgh: HMSO.

Scottish Pre-school Play Association (1990) *Code of Practice for SPPA Member Groups.* Glasgow: SPPA.

Scottish Pre-school Play Association (1992) *Facts and Figures.* Glasgow: SPPA.

Scottish Statistical Office (1992) *Provision for Pre-school Children*. Statistical Bulletin Education Series, Ref. EDN/A2/1992/11. Edinburgh: SSO.

Strathclyde Regional Council (1985) *Under Fives.* Report of the Member Officer Group. Glasgow: Strathclyde Regional Council.

Strathclyde Regional Council (1992) *Link-up for Under 6s and their Families.* Strathclyde Link-up Development Training Project. Glasgow: Strathclyde Regional Council.

Watt, J., Clark, H. and Smith, I. (1991) *Pilot Projects in Nursery Education in Grampian Region.* Report to the Regional Council of an evaluation of part-week nursery provision. Aberdeen: Department of Education, University of Aberdeen, mimeo.

Wilkinson, J. E., Kelly, B. and Stephen, C. (1993) *Flagships: an evaluation research study of community nurseries in Strathclyde Region, 1989-1992.* Glasgow: Department of Education, University of Glasgow.

CHAPTER 6

TRAINING FOR QUALITY IN EARLY EDUCATION

Annette Holman and Sue Kleinberg

Introduction

The project team which developed national vocational qualifications for those working with children under seven for the Care Sector Consortium (CSC, 1991), identified 27 different settings in which people commonly work with young children and their families. Increasing attention is being paid to the training needs of those working in these settings which we refer to as 'educare'. We have used that word because it reflects a dual concern for learning and well-being and covers common goals. All staff need training which equips them to provide both developmentally appropriate education and care.

In this chapter we focus on those who work in group settings in the public, private or voluntary sector. This commonly includes: day nurseries, family centres, children's centres, nursery schools, nursery classes, the early stages of primary school, playgroups, parent and toddler groups, crèches and play buses. Even this narrowed range of settings is complex. Within it one will find a range of staff with a variety of qualifications and remits and job titles will not necessarily give enough information about what is done in a specific setting. Here we put a greater emphasis on those employed by local authorities and on recent structural changes in their training.

The lack of a common training framework has made it difficult to talk about, let alone provide, training of an agreed quality. Attempts to depict visually the current opportunities for training open to workers with under-eights would resemble a child's first explorations with a pencil! No organisation has overarching responsibility for training and little attention has been paid in the past to ladders of opportunity which would enable workers to train for career progression in a flexible way. There has been neither a progressive coherent framework of qualifications for the wide range of workers with under-eights nor for those within any one occupational group.

Current changes in structures are beginning to grapple with this: first, through changes made with the intention of improving fitness for purpose in all training experiences; and second, through credit accumulation and transfer systems which, along with profiles of training, could lead to the construction of bridges between different career paths. The outcomes of such changes are likely to be the sharing of understanding from different perspectives and the building of common perspectives. Changes in structures provide conditions for quality educare, but they must be matched by a supportive workplace culture which values discussion about the relationship between quality in training and quality in practice.

Reviewing recent work on professional teacher development, Hargreaves and Fullan (1992) suggest four important aspects of a framework for conceptualising and understanding this aspect of training: the person, the purpose, the work context, and the culture of working relationships. The framework reminds us that it is people who develop practice: their personal and professional life histories, their values and perhaps their age, for example, will be influential in their judgment of quality.

For us, 'training' has too narrow a connotation. We consider 'education' and 'development' to be equally important concepts in relation to the quality of a workforce which relates to young children. We use the word 'training' as a shorthand reference for processes which develop the knowledge, skills and dispositions needed for understanding what is involved in 'educare', making judgments and carrying out good practice.

To illustrate developments, we look in turn at initial training for teachers, then at training for nursery nurses and others. We use five headings: *entry and routes; model of the job; course content; relationship to the workplace;* and *statements of quality.* We then discuss quality in these courses and elsewhere before looking at post-experience training. Finally we look to the future.

Initial Teacher Education (ITE)

Entry and routes

Five Colleges of Education in Scotland, now within or associated with five Universities, provide courses leading to the Teaching Qualification (TQ) Primary which covers the age range three to twelve years. Students with a first degree take the 36-week Postgraduate Certificate in Education (Primary). Students who enter with University entrance level qualifications take the four-year concurrent BEd degree. The BEd route has recently been opened up to those who have taken an access course deemed equivalent to university entrance qualifications. A small number, usually transferring from the secondary sector, will take the one term Additional TQ (Primary). There has recently been an increase in the recruitment of students with wider life experience than those following the traditional school to college route.

Model of the job

Primary courses have a shared view of the teacher as a

generalist who can work with any stage. The *pro* and *anti* arguments on age specialisation raised by Curtis and Hevey (1992) and on subject specialism (Gosden, 1989) have not really been an issue in Scotland.

Kirk (1988) notes that all the courses have conceptual frameworks which inform professional activities. Each highlights planning, implementation and evaluation and contextualises learning and teaching experiences. Most frameworks are based on the concept of a reflective practitioner who theorises, investigates, has an open approach, and systematically monitors educational activities and personal practice and values. The importance of the reflective stance as a goal for initial training is stressed by McIntyre (1993) .

Course content

Students take core curriculum studies in English Language, Mathematics, Environmental Studies, Expressive Arts, and Religious and Moral Education, reflecting the structure of Scottish 5-14 Curriculum Guidelines. Professional Studies deal with issues in human development, learning and teaching. Cross-curricular issues such as multi-cultural education and gender awareness are included, as are special educational needs and technology. In addition there are optional or elective courses.

Relationship to the work place

School experience is seen as central, and other college programmes relate their inputs to that experience. Two key developments have taken place in this field: first, a pre-five placement now obligatory for all students; and second, a new model of partnership with schools.

Pre-five experience in schools

Since the mid-eighties, courses have included pre-five school experience under the supervision of a teacher. In time there will be more primary teachers who, having had such a place-ment, might be expected to have a deeper understanding of the curriculum and concerns of educare. Such first hand experience should lead to richer conceptualisations of: continuity and progression; parental and community involvement; inter- and intra- professional liaison; team work; and the role of the adult in the development of the child's 'intelligences' and well-being, through the creation of learning environments and sensitive interactions.

If deeper understandings do develop this should benefit all children, particularly those in Primary 1 to 3. Boyle (1992) warns us that the discipline base and programmes of study of 5-14 Guidelines will need teachers who

> do not lose sight of the need to develop in pupils those skills which are pre-requisites for learning and which may not have been developed before entry to school. (p. 26)

and, further, that the 'central role' of parents

> requires analysis and definition in relation to the 5-14 development programme. (p. 25)

Experience of a pre-five placement enables future teachers to be better informed on these issues, giving them a broader perspective when debating the curriculum. The development of shared understandings to inform liaison and curricular continuity may require a lengthy period of time and experience of a range of settings. There are limits on both in initial teacher training (ITE). Furthermore, after qualifying, many teachers may not be within an early education environment for some considerable time after their first appointment.

The HMI inspection of school experience in primary BEd courses (SOED, 1991) noted that for pre-five placements

> the number of days ...... varied from 10 to 20 across the five colleges. (p. 9)

Whilst the duration can be longer where students are allowed to opt for a nursery placement in the later stages of their course, this is not common across courses, or commonly chosen. The time spent with this age group on the postgraduate certificate in education (PGCE) course is less but similarly ranges in its duration.

The Scottish Office Education Department's *Guidelines for Teacher Training Courses* (SOED, 1993) lay down conditions for the Primary Teaching Qualification (TQ) courses. They confirm the need for students to have experience

> with children who have not entered P1 in a nursery school or class, preferably under the guidance of a nursery teacher. (p. 6)

The word 'preferably' has caused concern. The practice and ideal is for supervision by an experienced teacher who has proficiency with the relevant age group. Given the uneven provision of nursery schools and classes, it remains to be seen if any courses will seek places in settings where there is not a teacher and how, if this happens, the development and assessment of the student's professional competences will be achieved.

The opportunity for students to work with an experienced primary teacher has become complex to manage because teachers move stages more frequently. Furthermore, the demise of the Assistant Head (Early Stages) post has removed a post in which resided leadership, advocacy and a voice of early education to which students had access.

The Scottish system shares with others a problem in ITE's capacity to give students first hand experience of the variety of educare provision available. Proposals for shared multidisciplinary courses such as a BA (Early Childhood) followed by a PGCE year, or specialisation by age in BEd degrees, both discussed in England, could be attractive to some students and employers despite the problems they pose for the generalist stance. It is unlikely that Scottish

teachers will want to move towards more specialisation in
ITE given their concerns about teacher education developments in England and Wales: the 'licensed' and 'articled'
routes and the now defunct proposals for a one-year course
of training for mothers and others who had recognised
experience of working with young children (the 'Mums'
Army'). Their reasons are also connected to employment
and career prospects. If, however, more specialisation does
not happen, expansion of the early years components in an
already packed generalist course is unlikely.

Partnership with schools

Partnership of colleges, schools and education authorities is to-day very much on the educational agenda. Models which emphasise the reflective practitioner and focus
on professional action imply that increased attention will
be given to placement experiences. One aspect of this is to
seek to integrate and value equally the contributions of
school and college staff. There is concern about a lack of
shared understanding of course models and unclear role
boundaries: Elder and Kwiaktowski (1992), for example,
point to the continued dominance of an apprenticeship
model. Stark's study (1993) however, suggests that whilst
the apprentice model is still strong, the reflective model is
growing. A challenge for training is to consider the needs
of the adult learner at various points in their course and in
different settings and to devise means which appropriately use the strengths of each model.

The 5-14 Guidelines place

> particular stress on the role to be played in training by
> the schools in which students are placed to gain practi-
> cal experience. (HMSO, 1993, p. 1)

That role includes the design and implementation of

courses and requires 'partner schools' to have a clear role in the assessment of performance. Any increase in the training tasks for the primary or nursery teacher causes more concern because the responsibility and workload involved in training the student falls centrally on the class teacher.

Training has been a gift from one generation to the next, but developments in England and Wales and a Scottish pilot study researched by Cameron-Jones (1993) and by Powney *et al* (1993) raise issues of the very real costs involved, in the training of teachers, in assessment and teaching time for students, in providing support, and in monitoring systems. Wilson, Secretary of SOED, has stated that

> for the longer term, ministers would expect that the funding effect would be cost-neutral as far as overall resources for the school and higher education sectors are concerned. (Wilson, 1993)

As a result, much of the debate will inevitably be taken up with the necessary topic of resources before it can move on to consider the nature of professional learning and its requirements.

Statements of quality

For the first time ITE Guidelines have been couched in terms of generic *competences*. Four sets of competences are identified: the subject and content of teaching; the class-room (communication, methodology, class management and assessment); the school; and professionalism. The statement that professional competences should be taken to refer not just to performance but to knowledge, under-standing, critical thinking and positive attitudes, as well as to practical skills, has removed some concerns which arise from narrower interpretations of the construct.

Training routes for those other than teachers

Entry and routes

Currently, the traditional route into certificated quali-fications for early years workers in Scotland is a two-year modular course validated by the Scottish Vocational Education Council (SCOTVEC). Courses are based in Colleges of Further Education and entrance criteria vary. Those who complete a menu of modules specified by the Scottish Nursery Nurses Board (SNNB) can apply to that Board for registration as a nursery nurse. However, the menu of modules does not cover the range of functions of many workers and many potential students who have family commitments find full-time attendance for study at a college difficult. The modular system has flexibility allowing early years workers such as playgroup workers to take modules out of the menu which are relevant to their own employment .

A new framework is now being put together which will provide training routes for individuals in employment, and those without, in the full range of educare settings. One route is college-based, the other work-based. To obtain a work-based qualification, students need access to assessment in approved work places and to be registered with a SCOTVEC approved assessment centre. These assessment centres can consist of one organisation, for example a school or voluntary organisation, or organisa-tions can form consortia for training purposes.

Initially, each route will have two consecutive levels of qualification, but it is envisaged that they should eventually be articulated with higher education to degree level. The new arrangements are driven by the development of Scot-tish Vocational Qualifications (SVQs) in childcare and education which have been available since January 1992.

Currently, most of those seeking a work-based award in childcare and education will gain it at Level II, this being the level for which most assessment centres have been granted recognition by SCOTVEC. Many candidates are being trained via employment schemes funded by Local Enterprise Companies.

The proposed framework is as follows:

Figure 1:   Child Care and Education

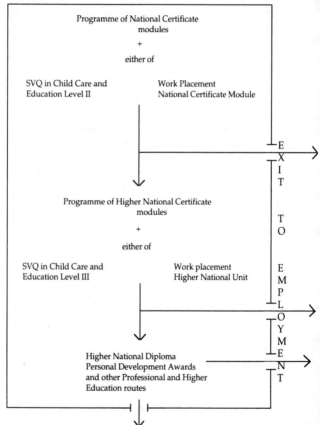

It is important to note the following points:

1. There is no time limit on the work-based route to an SVQ.

2. There is no requirement to take SCOTVEC modules in order to obtain an SVQ. Candidates have to demonstrate they have the necessary knowledge and understanding which underpins each unit and element of competence. How they obtain it is not prescribed.

3. The National Certificate (NC) and the Higher National Certificate (HNC) Programmes last for one academic year. The National Certificate is not a named award. Students have a Candidate's Record of Achievement which lists the units which have been successfully completed. The new National Certificate will be implemented in August 1994 and the Higher National Certificate in Childcare and Education in August 1995.

4. Although SCOTVEC validates and awards both the work-based and college-based routes to qualification, there are separate assessment systems.

5. It will be possible for candidates who have an NC or HNC to present themselves for accreditation for the relevant SVQ.

6. SVQ levels II and III in child care and education have an equivalent status to NVQs in child care and education in England, Wales and Northern Ireland.

7. The timetable for development of the framework beyond SVQ III and the HNC is unclear.

8. The Scottish Nursery Nurse Board (SNNB) has yet to make a statement about registration but it is likely that

SVQ level III/HNC will be the level of qualification needed for registration as a nursery nurse. Consideration is being given to according recognition, but not full registration, to those with an SVQ Level II or National Certificate.

Model of the job

The traditional nursery nurse training has been a two-year generalist course, preparing students for a range of jobs. In the voluntary sector, training on entry to the work is of much shorter duration and is focused on specific settings and topics such as the organisation of the playroom. The new framework includes the possibilities of some specialisation *via* the work-based route. The college-based routes remain generalist.

The SVQs in child care and education are based on a core and option-endorsement system. Any award will be endorsed with a subtitle which reflects a prescribed named pathway. At Level II there are four endorsements: *A. Work with Babies; B. Work in support of others; C. Work in a pre-school group; and D. Work in a community run pre-school group.* For Level III the five endorsements are: *A. Group Care and Education; B. Family Day Care; C. Pre-school Provision; D. Family Support;* and *E. Children with Special Needs.* (Endorsement A is more generalist than the others.)

A strength of the work-based route is that workers can acquire additional endorsements as their experience widens.

Course content

It is intended that all the underpinning knowledge and understanding for the SVQs will be covered by the new 'suites' of SCOTVEC National Certificate units and Higher

National units. At the time of writing this process is still underway .

National Certificate units to support the core content of knowledge required for a Level II SVQ will cover: child development, a range of health issues, play, children's behaviour, children with specific needs, equal opportunities, partnership with others, communication, and providing for an early years curriculum. The option-endorsements will be covered by content on care and feeding of babies, and on administration.

Higher National Certificate Units to support Level III will cover: child development at a more advanced level; how children learn; organising an educational environment; observation, recording and evaluation of assessment; child protection; social issues which affect families; children with special needs - again at a more advanced level; and anti-discriminatory practice. Endorsements will be covered by content on, for example, working with colleagues in a team, and involving parents in a pre-school setting.

Both certificates will have work placements in which students will have to demonstrate competence in the occupational standards developed for the SVQ at the relevant level.

Relationship to the workplace

In the new framework, placements continue to be essential to the development of student nursery nurses; in the work-based route it is obviously integral. Work -based training gives more opportunity for observing the development of children over time, recognising persistent patterns of behaviour, developing effective relationships with parents, working in a team, and dealing with unexpected consequences of plans.

College-based routes offer opportunities to gain experience in more than one setting. For young people who may be unsure as to which career path to take, the college-based route offers a broader view of provision and an appreciation, based on experience, of the relevance of principles of good practice across settings. For those in employment, placement in different settings may not be possible unless the employer has a reason to wish to broaden the employee's experience.

At least one local authority Social Work Department is already training employees to the new occupational standards independent of previous training. Social Work Departments are already familiar with the SVQ system because of their need to train residential staff, training for which government money is already available. However, when staff already possess an SNNB qualification or its equivalent, there may not be a strong incentive to retrain employees.

Discussion of course models has not received as much attention as it has in teacher training, but it is likely that the apprenticeship model will be particularly influential in the SVQ route. All the real, and until now hidden, costs of placement referred to previously occur in both routes.

Statements of quality

SVQs in child care and education were developed *via* a project team which included experienced early years practitioners and an academic who understood the field well. They were employed by the government-established Training Agency which was experienced in developing 'competence based' vocational qualifications using a methodology drawn from the principles of behaviourist psychology. The team on the other hand, reflecting the beliefs and practice of the field, took a holistic view in which 'process' as well as 'product' was seen to be important. They argued, correctly, that it is not enough to know how to carry out set tasks: knowing 'why' is also important and being able to explain the 'why' to a parent of a child or to a colleague is an integral part of the job. The work of the team resulted in a set of occupational standards issued by the Care Sector Consortium (1991).

One step taken to ensure that the framework for initial training reflected the approach of practitioners was to include at the beginning of the document containing the standards a declaration of the values, attitudes and principles which must be demonstrated in practice.

Quality

How is quality achieved in all these courses? Both ITE and newer courses emerging through SCOTVEC and FE colleges have systems for quality assurance and quality control. The former sets up standards and procedures for processes such as accreditation and validation which must be met before the route can be opened. The latter enables the detection of errors or problems through monitoring and inspection. It is also aimed to achieve quality through the involvement of external bodies such as the General Teaching Council (GTC), SCOTVEC, SOED and external examiners/verifiers and internal bodies such as Boards of Examiners and course review procedures.

A debate in both routes is about the relative weight to be given to functional competence and to the development of understanding and guiding principles. Both routes employ the term 'competences'. Each, however, puts caveats around that construct, taking the view that competence is necessary but is not sufficient to describe, design, regulate and inform practice in the education and care of young children. As Athey (1990) states:

> communication on high quality education requires professional knowledge. (p. 3)

The extent to which the conditions needed for fostering

such knowledge for understanding can be retained in some routes and established in others is a major question.

Understanding develops through reflection on experiences and takes time. Reflection is linked to ideas of purpose and purpose is linked to values and beliefs about what ought to happen. Reflection is essential to professional development and, despite its tranquil connotations, involves actively enquiring about what has been happening, establishing criteria for evaluating its worth, and considering whether or not there are lessons to learn for the future. Training, at whatever stage or by whatever route, should promote discussion with others including peers, tutors, and proficient practitioners.

No less important is the contribution made by research through its indirect promotion and examination of quality. This can be influential through its contribution to the evaluation of courses, to content (including the debate on what constitutes quality), and through access to research principles. There has been a welter of research evidence from studies relevant to educare, which is becoming embedded at different levels. The emerging consensus amongst practitioners on the broad principles for quality policy, provision and practice have been articulated in a range of publications including the Rumbold Report (DES, 1990) and those of the National Children's Bureau by Rouse (1991) and Cowley (1991). The work of Wells (1985), Tizard and Hughes (1984), Wolfendale (1989), Rogoff (1991), and Gardner (1991) are but a few which address specific topics in more detail and bridge the pre-five/primary gap. More research focusing on practitioners in action is, however, needed. As Brown and McIntyre (1993) say:

> an understanding of the nature of activity we call 'teaching' must be a priority. (p. 1)

The same point might be made about the skilful practice

of other occupations in the pre-five field about which there is a dearth of studies. Melhuish and Moss (1990), Moss and Melhuish (1991), Calder (1990) and Hutt *et al* (1989) touch on, but do not centrally address, the practitioner's world.

The mix of practical, theoretical and philosophically-based content needed by individual practitioners will vary. In the early stages, the novice may long for and need practice and practical knowledge simply to get through a day. Initial training is, therefore, likely to contain a high proportion of content which enables the job to be 'done'. The shorter the course the more likely this is to be the case. However, even in the early stages of learning, personal practice has to be considered in relation to its purposes.

Whilst we believe that in relation to quality, policy, provision and practice issues inter-relate, the major test for quality in training must lie in its relevance to practice. That requires a judgment and understanding of how worthwhile the content of what is being learned is to the child. It is through using knowledge of the connections between children's development and what they learn, how they are encouraged to learn, the environment in which learning is promoted, and an examination of outcomes for children, that quality will be furthered.

Moving into work

What training is available as a career progresses? Teaching, unlike the other occupations we have mentioned, has a mandatory two-year probationary period, and the GTC has recently tackled induction issues producing packs of materials for work with those newly in post (GTC, 1990). The increasingly frequent form of entry to employment by short-term contracts hampers plans for induction. Some local authorities, often linking with colleges, have been experimenting with support systems for probationer teachers by creating networks, reducing contact hours, and offering training inputs to try to meet their needs. Provision for other pre-five workers has been more *ad hoc* and largely depends on what is offered within the work place. For the voluntary sector, where workers may operate only one or two sessions per week, there are specific problems. The work of Draper *et al* (1992) and others, suggests that novices need a 'protected' period. They need to experience processes which have only been touched on in their initial training. The knowledge of children which can be achieved in a placement is limited; the rhythm of the year is rarely experienced. In teaching, a Professional Profile for Prospective Teachers (PPPT) is completed for all at the end of their course and forwarded to employers. One of its functions is to aid planning for support and development. Increasingly, work places identify an experienced colleague to 'mentor' or look after the novice, and 'welcome' or 'induction' packs which provide key information about the work, smooth the transition.

Moving work on

In house opportunities

Theoretically, a wide range of differing types of training are available to all early years workers: formal and informal; award-bearing and non-award-bearing; training open to individuals and to staff of whole establishments; open learning and 'direct contact' learning; and opportunities for which staff have volunteered, or been 'nominated' or which they have been obliged to take up. The reality is, however, that access to training outwith the work place is restricted. There are no rights to training and no formal 'rationing' of this scarce resource. For the voluntary sector, the problem of finance to fund training is particularly acute.

Professional development 'in -house' may well have the greatest impact on the practitioner. Development based in and on the work-place can address well the four dimensions of our framework: the purpose of the training; the individual person; the work context; and the culture of working relationships. It is here that issues of values and practice and their relationships can be addressed systematically and there is the time to build up expertise. Development activities are likely to be meaningful and purposeful and necessarily involve the self. When an in-house development culture exists, the perception of problems is more likely to initiate change.

In the work-place there are many developmental opportunities, other than through courses: shadowing, visits to other establishments, staff exchanges, group discussion, and participating as members of working parties are only a few examples. By these means an awareness and appreciation of the contributions of others grows, and feedback on new developments allows them to be monitored and evaluated. The work place also has the potential to be the site for research on both the activities of the group and the values which underpin them. This can be done either as part of an externally funded project but, perhaps more importantly, as an internal effort to examine what is happening in particular aspects of the group's work.

Currently, we see four innovations related to in-house training which we believe are benefiting practice. Many have developed within the context of centrally-funded government initiatives. Most are at very early stages in their life and are undocumented by research. They are: shared courses, curriculum development, training specifications and profiling.

Shared courses

These include courses where pre-five staff work alongside primary colleagues on management training modules and 5-14 curriculum activities, and courses which include staff from a range of settings. The sharing of courses does not necessarily mean the blurring of occupational or setting differences and is particularly useful for three kinds of topics: those which are generic to all settings – liaison, assessment, continuity of curricular experience, for example; those topics which are 'new' – specific policy initiatives on bullying, for example; and those which require inter-professional collaboration and teamwork.

Curriculum development

Curriculum development initiatives overlap with the activity generated by the 5-14 National Guidelines noted above. Many teachers have been involved in examining current practice as it relates to the Guidelines. This 'audit', we believe, has given more status to the role of language in learning and to diagnostic assessment. Recently a number of local authorities have generated guidelines for the early stages. These differ in the age range covered, some covering 0-5, others 3-5 or 3-8, and this may well have implications for curricular continuity and progression. What is important, however, is that these Guidelines are all documenting a child-centred, process-based approach, and that practitioners have been involved in the articulation of good practice. This has been a major professional development exercise for those involved. Many of the documents should provide support for those, in a variety of settings, who may need to keep early years principles alive in face of the pressures of the 5-14 curriculum reforms. The Guidelines, and the discussion generated by them, have been particularly welcome and needed, given the hiatus in curriculum development associated with the delay, and then non-publication, of the SED report on *Provision For Under Sixes*, as noted by Watt (1990). The recent (1994) publication from the Scottish Office *Education of Children Under 5 in Scotland* does not, in our view, take debate any further forward.

Other documents could be noted here: for example, the National Children's Bureau pack, *Developing a Curriculum for the Early Years* (NCB, 1989), and the Open University's *Working with Under Fives* (OU, 1991). Packs like these are 'user-friendly', employing video, audio and text to focus attention on research studies which might not otherwise be easily accessible. They also include a consideration of values. It is not clear how extensive an impact these initiatives have had on the voluntary sector but, for example in Strathclyde, the Early Years Voluntary Sector Forum has a sub-group which is concerned with curriculum matters and Strathclyde Region Education Department will be working in conjunction with the Forum to produce a booklet on the curriculum.

Training specifications

Our experiences and contact with local authority staff suggest that the process of development planning and, increasingly, the responses to the government's *Devolved School Management* (DSM) initiative have had a considerable impact. The former has involved educare staff in variations of the 'plan-do-review' cycle with all that involves in planning and reviewing their work comprehensively. By identifying development needs, constructing action plans and seeking evidence of their strengths and weaknesses, staff in pre-five establishments have been able to produce more finely-tuned specifications for courses. This has been of great importance in trying to overcome the problem of courses 'missing the mark'.

The DSM developments are also moving establishments to the position of 'purchasing' and prioritising training requirements. Given the perennially small budget for training, and the move to 'real costing' by major providers, an emerging practice is for clusters of establishments to purchase training together, or for one establishment to purchase it and then offer places to others. The prospect of early years workers coming together across settings and creating networks of common interests is an exciting one: it has great potential for strengthening everyone's understanding. Sharing practice can lead to greater wisdom and being able to tap the wisdom of others should improve the practice of everyone involved. These networks could include voluntary and private sector staff.

Profiling

The idea of individual professional development portfolios is increasingly discussed. The PPPT mentioned earlier, the *Portfolio of Work* used by teachers in the Staff Development and Appraisal initiative, and the SCOTVEC *Record of Achievement* are three such devices. Whilst there may be concerns about the compatibility of appraisal and development, as noted by Hickcox and Musella (1992), the potential of such profiles is worth considering. As more experiences are provided in-house, as credit transfer systems develop for award-bearing courses, and as the accreditation of learning gathers force, some structured way for recording accounts of training will become increasingly necessary.

It is a moot point whether in-house training activities will be able to balance informational and procedural aspects of policy with staff development on the implementation of that policy and its underlying values in practice. Collaboration will be the key. Some studies (Handy, 1985; Hargreaves and Fullan, 1992) suggest that development is best fostered by a collaborative workplace culture, exemplified by the way people work together, by mutual trust, openness, sympathy, tolerance of differences and leadership through example. Rowie Shaw, in an address to the Tong School Conference on school-based teacher training in Bradford (unpublished, 1993), described this in terms of the 'head as head learner'. Such a culture is rare, in part, as Hargreaves and Fullan (1992) suggest, because of limited time to plan together, and heavy curriculum demands which often limit discussion of development topics to

> routine advice giving, trick trading and material sharing. (p. 228)

Other factors such as union concerns, inadequate job descriptors, shift work, job sharing and staff turnover are also influential so that, even where planned activity time is built in to a system, it is seldom enough.

Out of house opportunities

The provision of training outwith establishments is changing in ways other than those noted above. For teachers some changes may be perceived negatively. The Froebel Certificate in Nursery and Infant Education and the College Associateship in Early Education have been dismantled. These offered one year full-time study and an opportunity to develop specialisation with three to eight-year-olds. Special Qualification courses in Infant or Nursery Education are still available in some Colleges. These are popular, practical and have been influential, not least in their 'use and custom' relationship to promotion in schools. They are, however, post-experience courses and are tending to be remodelled to fit postgraduate pathways.

Postgraduate pathways offer the opportunity to accumulate credits in the journey through Certificate and Diploma modules and on to a Masters degree. Early education pathways, with credit accumulation and transfer, along with the accreditation of prior learning experiences, are key features which promote flexibility. Diversity of routes is a marked feature of recent developments. Some schemes enable local authorities or others to have their courses accredited and validated within the higher education system.

The restructuring of award-bearing courses has retained the opportunity to specialise through named pathways in early education but has also opened up 'mix and match' routes. The named pathways require studies to be related to action in the workplace thereby strengthening the likelihood that changes in practice and understanding will benefit children and workplace realities will be fed into the course. While at one time a working party of the Scottish Committee for Staff Development in Education (SCOSDE) tried to produce national guidelines for post-qualifying courses for teachers, what we now face is the diversity of the marketplace. A new set of differences is emerging across Colleges of Education within similarly named courses: some routes are available to all occupational groups; some are oriented to the 0-8 age group, others to 3-8; some provide teachers with an Additional Qualification, and others do not.

For other early years workers there is only one certificated course at a higher level that has academic currency, namely the Higher National Certificate, *Working with Children in their Early Years*. It too requires studies to be related to the workplace. The future place of this HNC within the SCOTVEC system is under review. Other advanced certificated courses are not specifically targeted at early years work and an SNNB *Certicate in Post Qualifying Studies* suffered from its lack of articulation with other qualifications.

What limits all these training moves is cost: moves to twilight courses and distance learning are not just to open up access, they are in part driven by the problems of 'cover' costs for releasing staff. The move to self-funding or partial self-funding is not new, and is reported to us as growing in scale.

In-house and out-of-house opportunities

Whilst in-house concerns are increasingly framing developments in training and the work place is where change is tested, the devolution from centralised provision puts the onus for 'keeping up to date' on establishments. The uniqueness of the work-place is its strength but it is also a potentially limiting factor. Changes in the funding and organisation of training may well impair links with further and higher education, and the impending reorganisation of education authorities within local government reforms may have similar effects on links with advisory services. If links are lost, current practice may come to be taken as the yardstick for good practice, a stance which, in the long run, could be damaging to progress. If good practice is 'common-sense', then why reflection? 'Common-sense' may be slow to recognise and deal with wider societal issues which could and should affect policy and practice. If internal debate is not based on critical scrutiny, informed by outside ideas, the capacity to participate in quality assurance, let alone quality control, is diminished.

The future

What might impede the development of quality in training? As we see it, there are three main problem areas. First, if the philosophy which at the moment underpins much of the drive to competence becomes increasingly dominant, untempered by more 'human' values, not only training but practice will be set back. Second, lack of finance is likely to be a continuing bugbear. Third, there are many potentially adverse effects from local government reorganisation and there may well be a period in the immediate post-reorganisation phase when educational development will be given little attention.

On the positive side, however, we also see growth points. First, there is the emergence of more accessible and flexible ways of taking personal development forward, some of which can be certificated. Second, bridges are being constructed: between 'care' and 'education'; between the public, voluntary and private sectors; and between different kinds of training agencies. Third, there are clear signs that the value of in-house training is being increasingly recognised. Fourth, the impact of the Children Act (1989), with its mandatory triennial reviews and annual inspections will keep planning and quality on everyone's agenda. And finally, an increase in publications in the early years field – practice and policy guidelines as well as research findings – should help in focussing our attention on how and why children learn as well as what they learn. The extent to which professional development fosters such understanding is a key aspect of quality.

References

Athey, C. (1990) *Extending Thought in Young Children - a Parent-Teacher Partnership.* London: Paul Chapman.

Boyle, C. (1992) Early Education Into the 1990's *in Reflections on Curriculum Issues: Early Education.* Dundee: Scottish Consultative Council on the Curriculum.

Brown, S. and McIntyre, D. (1993) *Making Sense of Teaching.* Milton Keynes: Open University Press.

Calder, P. (1990) The training of nursery workers - the need for a new approach. *Children and Society*, 4 (3), 251-263.

Cameron-Jones, M. and O'Hara, P. (1993) *The Scottish Pilot PGCE (Secondary) Course, 1992-1993.* Edinburgh: Moray House Institute of Education, Heriot-Watt University, Edinburgh.

Care Sector Consortium (1991) *National Occupation Standards for Working with Young Children and Their Families.* London: HMSO.

Cowley, L. (1991) *Young Children in Group Day Care: Guidelines for Good*

Practice. London: National Children's Bureau.

Curtis, A. and Hevey, D. (1992) Training to Work in The Early Years, *in* Pugh, G. (ed.) *Contemporary Issues in The Early Years: Working Collaboratively For Children*. London: Paul Chapman.

Department of Education and Science (1990) *Starting With Quality:Report of the Committee of Inquiry into the Educational Experiences Offered to Three and Four year Olds* (Rumbold Report). London: HMSO.

Draper, J., Fraser, H. and Taylor, W. (1992) *A Study of Probationers*. Edinburgh: Moray House Institute of Education, Heriott-Watt University.

Drummond M. J., Lally, M. and Pugh, G. (eds) (1989) *Working With Children. Developing a Curriculum For the Early Years*. London: National Children's Bureau.

Elder, R. and Kwiatkowski, H. (1993) *Partnership in Initial Teacher Education*. Dundee: Northern College.

Gardner, H. (1991) *The Unschooled Mind*. New York: Basic Books

General Teaching Council for Scotland, (1990) *Report on the Management of Probation*. Edinburgh: General Teaching Council.

Gosden, P. H. J. H. (1989) Teaching Quality and the Accreditation of Initial Teacher-Training Courses, *in* McClelland, V. A. and Varma, V.P. (eds.) *Advances in Teacher Education*. London: Routledge.

Handy, C. B. (1985) *Understanding Organisations*. London: Penguin.

Hargreaves, A. and Fullan, M. G.(eds)(1992) *Understanding Teacher Development*. London: Cassell.

Hickcox, E. S. and Musella, D. F. (1992) Teacher performance, appraisal and staff development, *in* Fullan, M. and Hargreaves, A. (eds.) *Teacher Development and Educational Change*. London: The Falmer Press.

Hutt, S. J., Tyler, S., Hutt, C. and Christopherson, H. (1989) *Play, Exploration and Learning*. London: Routledge.

Kirk, G. (1988) *Teacher Education and Professional Development*. Professional Issues in Education 1, Edinburgh: Scottish Academic Press.

McIntyre, D. (1993) Theory, Theorizing and Reflection in Initial Teacher Education *in* Calderhead, J. and Gates, P. (eds.) *Conceptualizing Reflection in Teacher Development*. London: The Falmer Press.

Melhuish, E. and Moss, P. (eds.) (1990) *Day Care For Young Children: International Perspectives*. London: Routledge.

Moss, P. and Melhuish, E. (eds.)(1991) *Current Issues in Day Care For Young Children*. London: HMSO.

National Children's Bureau (1989) *Developling a Curriculum for the Early Years*. London: NCB.

Open University (1992) *Working With Under Fives*. PE 635. Milton Keynes: Open University Press.

Powney, J., Edward, S., Holroyd, C. and Martin, S. (1993) *Monitoring The Pilot. The Moray House Institute PGCE (Secondary)*. Edinburgh: Scottish Council for Research in Education.

Rogoff, B. (1991) *Apprenticeship in Thinking*. Oxford: Oxford University Press.

Rouse, D. (1991) *Babies and Toddlers: Carers and Educators.Quality For Under Threes*. London: National Children's Bureau.

SOED (1991) *The Arrangements for School Experience in Scottish Primary B.Ed Courses*. HM Inspectors of Schools Report. Edinburgh: Scottish Office Education Department.

SOED (1993) *Guidelines for Teacher Training Courses*. Edinburgh: HMSO.

SOED (1994) *Education of Children Under 5 in Scotland*. Edinburgh: SOED.

Stark, R. (1993) *School Experience in Initial Primary School Teacher Training: A Study of the School Experience Component in the Fourth Year of the Bachelor of Education Degree course at the University of Strathclyde*. Glasgow: University of Strathclyde, Jordanhill Campus.

Tizard, B. and Hughes, M. (1984) *Young Children Learning: talking and thinking at home and at school*. London: Fontana.

Watt, J. (1990) *Early Education:The Current Debate*. Professional Issues in Education 9. Edinburgh: Scottish Academic Press.

Wells, G. (1985) *Language Development in the Pre-school Years*. Cambridge: Cambridge University Press.

Wilson, G. (1993) *Text of the keynote address to the seminar on Partnership in Initial Teacher Training*. Edinburgh: Scottish Office Education Department.

Wolfendale, S. (1989) *Parental Involvement: Developing Networks Between School, Home and Community*. London: Cassell.

CHAPTER 7

THE ASSESSMENT OF QUALITY IN EARLY EDUCATION

J. Eric Wilkinson and Christine Stephen

Defining quality

This chapter examines the complex issues involved in assessing the quality of early years educational provision and practice. The analysis focuses exclusively on quality in the pre-five sector largely because of the considerable structural differences between this sector and formal primary schooling even though the term 'early education' often refers to the education of children in the age range 0-8.

The Shorter Oxford English Dictionary uses the term 'grade of excellence' as one of the defining characteristics of the word 'quality'. This concurs with everyday usage as a word denoting something of worth, something to be valued and highly respected. It is a word that has very wide application. However, the nature of exactly what is to be valued and respected is dependent on both the *context* within which quality is sought and the identification of the important *features* of such a context.

The context for this chapter is the education that takes place in nurseries - nursery schools, nursery classes, community nurseries, day nurseries *etc* – not only for the reason that the authors have had recent experience in examining matters pertaining to quality in such contexts (Wilkinson *et al*, 1993; Stephen and Wilkinson, 1994) but that the important features of this context are substantially different from the features of other educational contexts.

Quality is now an important matter in most public services and has reached a status commensurate with the 'jewel in the crown'. Such terms as 'Quality Assurance' are relatively new buzz words but they are not restricted to education. The basis for this emphasis on quality stems, in part, from government concerns, both in Europe and USA, to ensure that public money is prudently spent to obtain a better standard of service for those individuals and groups using such services: health, social services and education.

As far as educational provision for the under-fives is concerned, official recognition of the importance of quality was given in the House of Commons report of the Education, Science and Arts Committee in 1988. Although the report failed to address the problems of defining quality, it specified factors which contribute to quality in pre-five provision. Based on this all-party report, the Government set up the Rumbold Committee to examine the quality of educational experience which should be offered to three and four-year-olds. The Committee considered the needs of young children, and outlined a suitable curriculum and ways of implementing the curriculum. It also attended to the recording of children's progress, the need to review the provision and the education, training and support available for adults working in early years education. All of these aspects influence the quality of the child's experience. The Rumbold Report (DES, 1990) urged an increased concern with the quality of provision and proposed ways in which improvements in quality could be achieved and monitored.

The concern for quality also stems from a growing body of knowledge which demonstrates that children's development is markedly affected by different levels of quality in provision (Phillips *et al*, 1987).

Scarr and Eisenberg (1993), reviewing recent advances in child care research, outlined the most commonly agreed features of child care quality:

> health and safety;
> relationships between staff and children;
> a developmentally appropriate curriculum;
> limited group size;
> age appropriate staff ratios;
> adequate indoor and outdoor space; and
> adequate staff training.

However, there is no agreement as to the degree of emphasis to be given to each of these features. At a National Children's Bureau seminar focusing on quality provision for under- threes in 1990, three aspects of quality were addressed: the quality of relationships between adults and children; the quality of space, equipment and resources; and the quality of learning experiences for the child. Clearly, therefore, an important consideration in examining 'quality' is the relationship between children's development and the nature of the provision.

But children themselves are not the only group to be considered in the 'quality' debate. Quite rightly Balageur *et al* (1991) in their report to the European Commission identify two further sets of perspectives on quality: those of young parents, and those of professionals. To quote from Balageur *et al*:

> Parents are not a homogeneous group. Although they may have common interests, they are as individual as their children. A parent may have different criteria from professionals. For example she may consider maintaining family income as a priority for family stability and therefore seek day-care whereas professionals may argue that other forms of care are more appropriate for her child. Parents from a black community may feel strongly that white professionals do not fully understand the pressures and oppressions that their children

experience. A parent might have a decided view about gender-about the right way to bring up boys and girls-which conflicts with professional opinion. There may be differences about discipline and if and how children should be punished. Professionals sometimes argue that by virtue of their training and experience they have the best interests of the child at heart, and are in a better position to judge than parents what is best. (Balageur *et al*, 1991, p. 6)

Just as important as the attitude and belief system of parents is the professional perspective of the care givers, teachers and nursery nurses, in the nursery. A comprehensive assessment of quality must therefore take account of all these factors.

A further area of concern in the quality debate focuses on the tension between promoting quality and monitoring quality. Both Clarke-Stewart (1991) and Harms and Clifford (1980) have argued in favour of setting and monitoring indicators of quality, whereas Balageur *et al* (1991) have argued in favour of promoting quality:

Our broader aim is to engender discussion and provide a focus for debating high quality services, to look at what we might try to achieve to put our beliefs and our values about children into practice. (p. 8)

Balageur *et al* proposed ten categories of quality indicators:

- accessibility and usage
  eg admission priorities
       flexibility of nursery
       routines

- the community
  eg use of local facilities
       and resources

- environment
  eg safety
       nutrition of food
       space

- valuing diversity
  eg gender
       disability
       ethnic minorities
       other special needs

- learning activities
  eg range of activities
      curriculum planning
      materials

- assessment
  eg observation of children's
      records

- relationships
  eg adult-child relationships
      play

- cost benefits
  eg management of resources
      staff recruitment

- parent's views
  eg welcoming to parents
      information to parents
      involvement in management

- ethos
  eg self confidence
      happiness of children
      and staff evaluation

Balageur *et al* went on to examine the action that needs to be taken by authorities in ensuring that services meet the specific quality indicators and concluded:

> The most successful and far reaching quality assurance occurs when the government supports, endorses and encourages - but does not control - local initiatives. (p. 21)

Assessing quality in public services is now a major issue. In recent years, British governments have attempted to improve the delivery of public services in terms of their quality rather than their quantity. Value for money is now a fashionable slogan. However, not only have criteria to be established in the light of the service being provided, but the means of measuring and monitoring these criteria have also to be formulated. There are usually two approaches to this issue. Either one can adopt a *qualitative* approach using the subjective judgments of experts or one can adopt a *quantitative* approach based on specific instruments or scales. The former approach, which is the approach used by HMI when conducting a school inspection, has the advantage of being more comprehensive and detailed, but it is open to bias and dispute and, in the case of the HMI inspections, only conducted at very infrequent intervals. The quantitative approach, however, is more restricted and inflexible but is more objective and rigorous.

In any assessment of the quality of the services offered, it is necessary to reflect on the purpose of the assessment. If the purpose is essentially concerned with research and/ or evaluation it is necessary to examine quality by means of an objective tool which can be applied with reliability and validity. If, on the other hand, the purpose of the assessment is for promotion of quality *in situ*, a less rigorous instrument can be used as part of an overall strategy based on self-evaluation (Wilkinson and Stephen, 1992).

Measuring quality

A number of commercially available instruments now exist to assess the quality of the nursery environment. *The Early Childhood Environment Rating Scale* (Harms and Clifford, 1980) was developed to give an overall picture of the surroundings that have been created for the children and adults who share an early childhood setting. Environment, as it is used in this context, refers to the physical environment, the care routines, the learning experiences, the daily programmes and interactions with adults that a child experiences within some pre-five provision. The needs of adults working in that provision are also examined and account is taken of the level of parental involvement with the childcare environment.

The Harms and Clifford Scale consists of seven subscales which examine particular areas of provision:

> personal care routines for children;
> furnishings and display for children;
> language/reasoning experiences;
> fine/gross motor activities;
> creative activities;

social development; and
adult needs.

Unfortunately the Harms and Clifford Scale does not
include a specific dimension on curricular matters.

The ratings on any one subscale or dimension are
derived from the ratings on a number of separate items
that pertain to that dimension. For example, the rating on
the *personal care routines* dimension is the sum of ratings on
five separate items: greeting/departing; meals/snacks;
nap/rest; diapering/toileting; personal grooming.

Each item is rated on a seven-point scale ranging from
1 (inadequate provision) to 7 (excellent provision). The
points on the scale are clearly and closely defined so that
observation of the provision will readily result in one or
other rating being decided upon. For instance, for a
rating of 5 (good) on the 'room arrangement' item there
must be:

three or more interest centres defined and conveniently
equipped (Example - water provided, shelving adequate).
Quiet and noisy areas separated. Appropriate play space
provided in each centre (Example - rug or table out of the
flow of traffic). Easy visual supervision of centres.

After summing the item ratings given on any one subscale, a profile can be drawn charting the rating given on
that occasion for all the subscales or dimensions (see
Figure 2 for an illustration). The scores on each subscale
are plotted on the chart and the points connected to arrive
at the profile.

The Harms and Clifford scale has been subjected to two
forms of validity testing. First, independent experts rated
each item in the scale for its importance to childcare
provision. Second, the scale was applied to pre-five provision of varying quality by trainers familiar with the environments and by expert observers. When ratings on the
scale made by expert observers were compared with the

trainers' ratings on 18 playrooms, a rank order correlation of 0.74 was obtained. The results on both these tests support the validity of the scale: the scale does indeed measure variations in the quality of the environment for the child. Further tests were carried out to examine the reliability of the scale, its ability to produce consistent results. Inter-rater reliability was examined for the results obtained across playrooms (r = 0.88) and on individual items (r = 0.93). The internal consistency of the scale was also examined (standard *alpha* = 0.86). The results on these tests suggest that the scale can be used consistently across environments.

Although the Harms and Clifford Scale was developed in USA, it is applicable to nurseries in Britain. However, as previously intimated, the scale has a number of shortcomings, not least the absence of items examining the quality of the curriculum. A modified form of the scale has been developed by McCail (1991) for use in nurseries in Scotland. McCail extended the Harms and Clifford Scale into nine subscales:

> policy and managing;
> adult co-operation;
> language and reasoning experiences;
> creative activities;
> investigation;
> fine and gross motor activities;
> social/emotional development;
> personal care routines; and
> appropriate standard in premises and furnishings

McCail retained the seven-point scale for each item originally used by Harms and Clifford. Each of the nine subscales contained between five and ten items. Unfortunately, no reliability or validity data is available for McCail's adaptation of Harms and Clifford. However, this does not necessarily imply that it is not reliable or valid. Many teachers in nurseries in Scotland will find it a useful self-evaluation tool which will help in monitoring quality standards in their nursery.

Another useful instrument is the *Assessment Profile for Early Childhood Programs* (Abbott-Shim and Sibley, 1987). The Profile is a structured observation guide designed to assist in the process of self-assessment, identifying those aspects of a programme that positively contribute to children's development and identifying those aspects that require change.

Systematic self assessment is a process for improving the quality of early childhood programs. (p.3)

The instrument consists of structured observation checklists with different *components* targeted at different age groups: infants (0-2), pre-school (2-5) and school-age (5+). Within each component there are a number of *dimensions* with each dimension containing a set of *standards* based on values and expectations. Each standard is supported with specific *criteria* which are concrete, observable procedures, behaviours and records that exemplify the standards. As with the Harms and Clifford, the outcome is a profile graph across each of the dimensions.

The pre-school dimensions are: safety and health; learning environment; interacting; and individualising. An example of a Standard and associated Criteria is given in Figure 1.

Figure 1:   An Example from the Assessment Profile for Early Childhood
             Programs (Abbott-Shim and Sibley, 1987, p.13)

Component - Dimension - Standard - Criteria -	Pre-school
	   Interacting
	
	A. Teacher initiates positive interactions with children
	
	   1. Teacher initiates positive gestures (such as smiles, hugs and pats, holds).
	
	   2. Teacher initiates positive verbal interactions (such as praise and acknowledgement).
	
	   3. Teacher engages children in laughter and smiling through verbal exchanges and/or playful games and activities.
	
	   4. Teacher shares personal feelings and/or experiences as related to the activities of the day.

Abbott-Shim and Sibley also specified the nature of the advanced planning and preparation that is required before using the Profile. The essential features of this planning process are:

identification of suitable observers working in pairs;
training of the observers;
a staff meeting to discuss the purpose and plans of the assessment;
arrangements for the collection of data; and
a clearly defined feedback process.

Assessing quality in practice

Comparing Provision

As part of a recent study (Wilkinson *et al*, 1993) into new forms of pre-five provision in Strathclyde Region, the authors extensively used the Harms and Clifford Scale to compare the quality of the nursery environment in several nurseries on a longitudinal basis. In 1985, the Region issued a major policy statement on provision for children from birth to five (Strathclyde Regional Council, 1985). The report endorsed the concept of 'community nursery' referred to by Penn (1992) as

the flagships of the Council's philosophy on pre-fives.

Harms and Clifford ratings were used to address two crucial questions:

how did the quality of provision in the community nurseries compare with that in a good, conventional well-established nursery school?

and

is the quality of provision affected by external and internal factors?

An extra dimension was developed by the authors and added to those on the Harms and Clifford Scale using the same scaling methods. This extra dimension was concerned with the operation and extent of curriculum planning and the way in which this planning was implemented.

It was also possible, because of the interactive design of the study, to throw some light on the use of the Harms and Clifford Scale as a development tool, allowing some examination of the way in which staff in the nurseries reacted to feedback of 'quality' ratings. Each nursery room in the two community nurseries and two conventional nursery schools were observed using the Harms and Clifford ratings on three separate occasions, at approximately six-monthly intervals, Spring 1991, Autumn 1991 and Summer 1992. The researchers developed a standard procedure for conducting the observations and reporting back to the nurseries. In each case the observers, working in pairs, aimed to observe the environment avoiding conversations or activities taking place in the nursery. While the children readily appeared to accept the presence of external observers, in general paying little attention to them, staff were initially less comfortable.

The profiles obtained from each nursery were charted together to allow comparisons between nurseries at any one point in time. Examining the profiles obtained early in the development of the community nurseries in Spring 1991 (Figure 2) showed all the nurseries to be operating around the mid-point or above on the Harms and Clifford Scale with one of the long-established nursery schools offering a high quality of provision (as defined on the scale) clearly above that of the others. The chart showing the profiles obtained on the third rating, Summer 1992 (Figure 3) showed the new community nurseries to be operating at a level not too dissimilar from that in the nursery schools. While the two conventional nursery schools were still high on the ratings, this was matched in some subscales by the newer community nurseries, both of which demonstrated a noticeable move over time towards the 'excellent' end of the range. On the basis of this evidence, and the more detailed reports written to accompany the profiles, the researchers felt able to respond in relation to the first question posed, that community nurseries could offer a high quality environment which compared favourably with that in conventional nursery schools.

Turning to the ratings for particular nurseries over the period of the research, the vulnerability of quality to internal and external pressures was demonstrated. In one community nursery an identifiable deterioration in quality took place between the first rating in Spring 1991 and the second in Autumn 1991. Figure 4 shows a decline in the ratings on three subscales: *fine and gross motor activities, creative activities* and *social development.* The period from March to October 1991 was one of considerable tension amongst staff arising from acute accommodation problems and a number of staff changes. Furthermore, a new intake of children to the nursery in this period greatly increased the number of children with social and emotional behaviour problems, which itself contributed to stress in the nursery. Some retrieval in quality had occurred by the time of the third assessment, reflecting concerted efforts of staff to examine the curriculum offered and amend their practice.

The other community nursery also demonstrated that good facilities and equipment can enhance quality and that problems with the physical nature of a building can have a limiting effect on the quality of provision on particular sub-scales. The profiles obtained from the ratings (Figure 5) revealed consistently good ratings for *furnishings and display, fine and gross motor activities* and *creative activities.* The furnishings provided reflected the nursery's position as a newly renovated environment. It was well provided with equipment designed to promote children's fine and gross motor skills and good outdoor and indoor space was available for physical play. The systematic observation and rating of the environment available to children revealed other dimensions where the same quality was not found, for example, in the limited nature of the *language and reasoning* experiences recorded in Spring 1991 and the lower rating obtained on *social development*. Scores on the *personal care routines* sub-scale were consistently lowered by the nature of the building, specifically the siting of the toilet for children at some distance from the playroom.

While changes to improve quality may require a staff group to examine curriculum practice, it may also lead to more specific or small-scale changes which can, nevertheless, improve or enhance the quality of the environment provided for children. An example of this arose at one of the nursery schools in the study where comments on the provision of 'snacks' in a report accompanying the profile led to a significant change in the way in which snacks were prepared and served. This change was reflected in a subsequent improvement in the rating given on the *personal care routines* subscale.

Figure 2: Harms and Clifford Profiles (Spring, 1991)

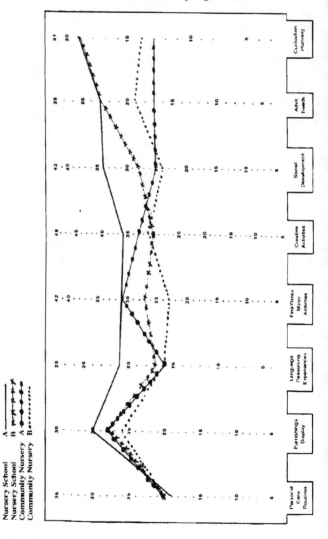

Nursery School   A
Nursery School   B
Community Nursery   A
Community Nursery   B

Figure 3: Harms and Clifford Profiles (Summer 1992)

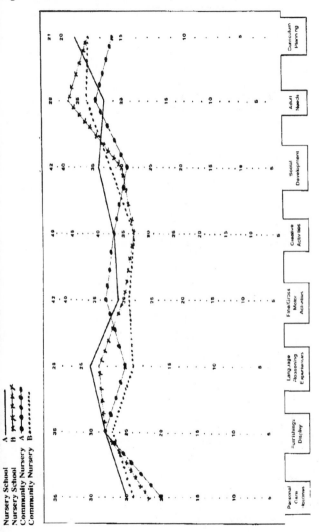

Nursery School   A
Nursery School   B
Community Nursery   A
Community Nursery   B

Figure 4: Harms and Clifford Profiles (Community Nursery A).

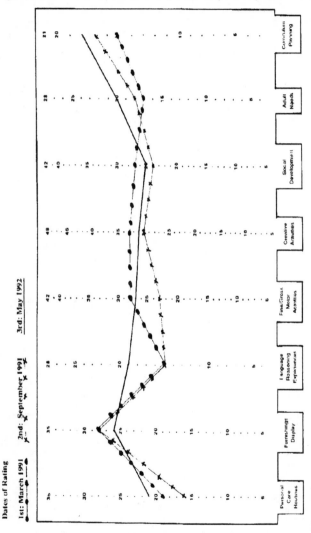

Figure 5: Harms and Clifford Profile (Community Nursery B)

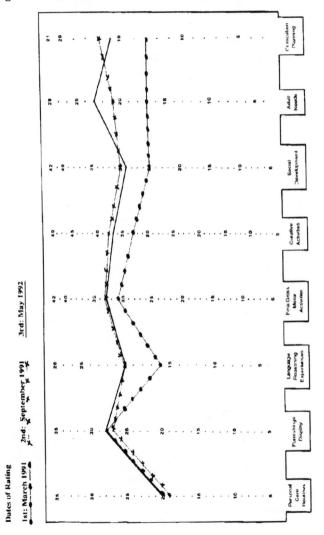

Identifying Training Needs

As well as allowing for comparisons to be made between nurseries and across time (both for research and staff development) the use of a standardised rating scale allows training needs to be identified from observations of practice. In a functional audit of day nurseries (Stephen and Wilkinson, 1994) designed to identify training needs in child care services offered by an English local authority Social Services Department, the Harms and Clifford Scale was used to identify the specific aspects of poor quality provision which training could address.

Poor quality provision was most commonly found with regard to *language and reasoning experiences, creative activities* and *social development.* The provision of activities designed to develop the understanding of language and the use of language was rated as inadequate at one day nursery (see Figure 6). The provision of opportunities to promote the development of reasoning skills and concepts was also rated as inadequate. At another nursery the quality of staff interaction in the language and reasoning activities limited the quality of rating given. At this same nursery, while some equipment was available for creative activities, it was not used daily or in a planned manner. The informal language used by staff to children at one nursery was given a poor rating as it was used largely to control behaviour.

These nurseries had had no curriculum development advice or training, a fact reflected in the quality of the environment they offered to the children. Problems also existed with the physical nature of the buildings and the equipment provided, both of which reduced the quality of children's experience. At one centre, for instance, the observers noted that no space was available for gross motor play indoors and the equipment available was minimal. As physical play could only take place outside, the scheduling of this kind of play was dependent on the weather. At another centre there were good facilities for routine care but poor furnishings for learning activities and relaxation. The arrangement of furnishings within the rooms was also poor, and child-related displays were considered minimal. It is interesting to note that at one of the two nursery schools also included in the study the traditional curriculum oriented sub-scales (*language and reasoning, fine and gross motor activities and creative activities*) were rated as providing a better quality experience than were the dimensions for *social development* and *provision for adult needs.*

The Harms and Clifford scale was particularly revealing in the sections of the nurseries devoted to 'baby care' that is, generally, care for children under the age of two years. (An alternative version of the scale was used to consider provision for babies.) One nursery offering day-care for babies was found to have a quality of environment (both physical and in terms of care and activities) that was unsatisfactory on all sub-scales. The other centres offering day-care for babies received ratings which varied with the differing dimensions, having generally good or adequate opportunities. The provision pertaining to *language and reasoning experiences* and to *creative activities* was, however, of generally poor quality. This finding mirrors that in Strathclyde community nurseries where a satisfactory curriculum for the youngest children had not been achieved. Curricular planning for those working with babies was one obvious training need identified in the day nursery audit.

Limitations of the quantitative approach to quality assessment

The studies described above illustrate the application of a quantitative approach to measuring quality. Clearly such a technique is valuable in a research context as it provides a data base from which systematic comparisons can be made. However, there are a number of limitations arising from the use of a standard scale and the observa-

Figure 6: Harms and Clifford Profile (Day Nursery)

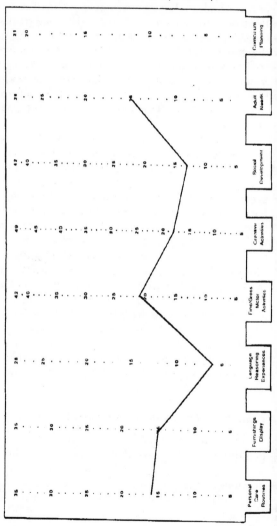

tion-based technique.

The first issue concerns the problem of the *representativeness* of the observations made. While researchers may do all they can to arrange for observations to be made in such a way as to maximise their representativeness, they are often reliant on the goodwill of staff and managers for access to childcare centres and freedom to observe. It is an often heard complaint of child care staff that the observations took place on a 'bad day'. Discussions as to why the day was not typical, and the impact that this had on the quality observed, can inform both research and staff development. It will also be obvious to all who work with young children that events, behaviour and emotions amongst children are unpredictable and make the notion of a 'typical' day difficult to maintain. Aiming to portray the quality of the environment experienced by a child on a 'representative' day rather than a 'standard' day is a more realistic goal.

Children in the playrooms generally show little interest in the observer and can easily be encouraged to participate in activities designed for them rather than continue to seek attention from the observer or behave in a way which will inhibit observation. The childcare staff, on the other hand, are more likely to be self-conscious and feel uncomfortable when an observer is present. Experience suggests that these feelings are quickly overcome by the demands of their task (attending to children) and can be further reduced by careful explanation of the purpose and procedure of the observation, giving staff the opportunity to become familiar with the scale and agreeing on the feedback procedures. These strategies can encourage positive reactions amongst staff towards the assessment of quality.

A further set of qualifications about the use of a standard scale must relate to the scale itself. There is no unambiguous and widely agreed statement as to what constitutes high or low quality in pre-school environ-

ments. There are, however, principles regarding the cur
riculum and the approach to child-care on which there i
a large measure of agreement. There will, nevertheless, be
some aspects of any scale which reflect the particular
perspective of those who compiled it. There may also be
cultural differences between practice in different social
and national circumstances. Any scale will, to some extent,
reflect the values and culture of those who devise it and, as
such, it is possible that both those using the scale and those
being assessed by it may consider some items inappropriate or irrelevant.

Having considered the implications of these qualifications and the limitations which they impose does not,
however, preclude the use of a quantitative approach to
assessing quality, although the limitations need to be
addressed within the context of each particular application or use of the scale in question. The use of a quantitative scale allows for questions about the quality of children's experience in a particular setting and the way in
which a centre functions to be addressed systematically.
Further, it allows for comparison both between and within
centres, for training needs to be identified and for the
strengths and weaknesses in a varied service provision to
be described. Using a scale like the Harms and Clifford
scale accompanied with detailed comments, allows for the
issue of quality in provision to be promoted in staff
development.

Quality assurance

Most local authorities in Scotland now implement
schemes of Quality Assurance for all their nurseries and
schools. Strathclyde Region is no exception. Strathclyde
was one of the first local authorities in Scotland to introduce such a scheme following the adoption of the
INLOGOV report in 1989.

As part of the scheme, the Region has generated a set of Mission Statements for each sector of the education system (SRC, 1992). The mission statement in each sector consists of Strands. Across each sector there are seven strands which consist of obligations on the part of the authority for:

provision of a full range of courses and services;
provision of opportunities for all individuals to achieve their full potential;
the supplying of suitable premises and resources;
encouragement of access to education throughout life;
fostering of genuine partnership in education;
the promotion of equal opportunity and social justice; and
supporting economic growth and prosperity.

Each strand is supported by a Quality Pointer. An example of such a pointer is shown in Figure 7 together with its relevant indicators.

Figure 7 An example of Pointers in the Pre-Fives Mission Statement of Strathclyde Regional Council

Quality pointer 5.2: Partnership with parents

5.2.1   Parents are made aware of the aims of the establishment
5.2.2   Parents are given advice on how to help with their children's learning and development
5.2.3   Parents are informed about their children's progress
5.2.4   Opportunities are given for parents to discuss their children's progress
5.2.5   The establishment liaises with parents about the needs of individual children
5.2.6   Parents are encouraged to take part in the life of the establishment
5.2.7   Parents are informed and, where appropriate, consulted about establishment matters including the curriculum
5.2.8   General information for parents is available in relevant community languages
5.2.9   The establishment is sensitive to the needs of parents
5.2.10 Where established, home visiting programmes are planned in partnership with parents

The Region employs a small number of inspectors to conduct the Quality Assurance assessment in selected nurseries. Data relevant to each Quality Pointer is generated either from available statistical material in the nursery or by direct observations and interview. On the basis of the data, a report is produced and shared with the head of establishment.

Whilst the virtue of the process is the openness of the criteria being used to judge quality levels, the drawback is the limitation of staff time to conduct the assessment. Each inspection takes at least a full week of time from inspectors often working in pairs or threes. In such a situation, all nurseries cannot rely on regional inspection to undertake quality assessments.

Wider perspectives in quality assessment

Two critical issues are pertinent to the assessment of quality in any educational institution: *accountability* and *professionalism*. Increasingly government bodies, both central and local are interested in promoting quality, the provision of effective services at a fair cost. It is now, rightly, the responsibility of those who run services to demonstrate to the employing authorities and to the wider public that effort is being made to promote and maintain a quality service. One way to contribute to this process of accountability is to conduct assessments of quality. Given that all educational establishments in Scotland now have to produce development plans which include a statement of aims and objectives, it is reasonable to expect each establishment to engage in reflection on how such aims and objectives are being achieved and to what degree. To inform this process of reflection it would not be unreasonable to expect schools and other institutions to generate data on the quality of their provision and practice. Indeed, given the requirement on local authories under the Children Act (1989) to register private nurseries, conducting assessments of quality would help s to enhance the level of provision in such nurseries.

Turning to the notion of professionalism, Kirk (1988) sees self-evaluation as a necessary commitment on the part of teachers:

> In the portrayal of teaching as a professional activity ....
> there has been repeated reference to the idea of the
> teacher as a self-monitoring and self-critical agent. (p. 14)

n other words, it is the responsibility of the trained professional to reflect on team practice in a systematic way. Part of this process, which was also recommended by the Rumbold Report, requires staff to be aware of how their own establishment measures up to specified quality standards.

One means of doing this could be to form 'clusters' of nurseries as, for example, exist in some areas of Strathclyde Region centred on an admissions panel. Heads of nurseries could then work in pairs to conduct quality assessments using say, the Harms and Clifford Scale, in nurseries in the cluster. How the information generated by this process was employed would be crucial. Many nursery staff might feel threatened by the general availability of quality profiles. Nevertheless, such profiles could form the basis of a formal staff development programme and thereby enhance the effectiveness of the provision.

> That notion of the endless quest for improved performance ...... is meaningless without the patient and unswerving commitment to self-scrutiny and the resourcefulness to act in the light of that self-scrutiny. (Kirk, 1988, p. 15)

References

Abbott-Shim, M. and Sibley, A. (1987) *Assessment Profile for Early Childhood Programs.* Atlanta, GA: Quality Assist.

Balageur, I. , Mestres, J. and Penn, H. (1991) *Quality in Services for Young Children* Brussels: Commission of the European Communities.

Clarke-Stewart, A. (1991) Day Care in the USA, *in* Moss, P. and Melhuish, E. (eds.) *Current Issues in Day Care for young Children*. London: HMSO

Department of Education and Science (1990) *Starting with Quality, Report of the Committee of Enquiry into the Quality of the Education Experience Offered to 3- and 4-year olds.* (The Rumbold Report). London: HMSO

Harms, T. and Clifford, R. M. (1980) *Early Childhood Environment Rating Scale.* New York: Teacher's College Press.

House of Commons (1988) *Educational Provision for the Under Fives,* Vol. 1. London: HMSO.

Kirk, G. (1988) *Teacher Education and Professional Development.* Edinburgh: Scottish Academic Press.

McCail, G. (1991) *Pre-Five Environment Quality Rating Scale.* Edinburgh: Moray House House College of Education.

Penn, H. (1992) *Under Fives - The view from Strathclyde.* Edinburgh: Scottish Academic Press.

Phillips, D., McCartney, K. and Scarr, S. (1987) Child Care Quality and Children's Social Development, *Developmental Psychology* 23 (4) 537-543.

Scarr, S. and Eisenberg, M. (1993) Childcare Research: Issues, Perspectives and Results, *Annual Review of Psychology,* 44, 613-44.

Stephen, C. and Wilkinson, J. E. (1994) A functional audit of training needs in local authority day care provision, *Local Government Policy Making* 20, 3.

Strathclyde Regional Council (1985) *Under Fives.* Glasgow: Strathclyde Regional Council .

Strathclyde Regional Council (1992) *Quality in Education - Pre-Fives.* Glasgow: Strathclyde Regional Council.

Wilkinson, J. E. and Stephen, C. (1992) *Evaluating Ourselves.* Glasgow: Department of Education, University of Glasgow.

Wilkinson, J. E., Kelly, B. and Stephen, C. (1993) *Flagships: an evaluation research study of community nurseries in Strathclyde 1989 - 1992.* Glasgow: Department of Education, University of Glasgow.